Privacy and Data Protection Law in Israel

Privacy and Data Protection Law in Israel

Michael Birnhack
Omri Rachum-Twaig

This book was originally published as a monograph in the International Encyclopaedia of Laws/Privacy and Technology Law.

Founding Editor: Roger Blanpain
General Editor: Frank Hendrickx
Volume Editors: Jos Dumortier, Pieter Gryffroy, Ruben Roex & Yung Shin Van Der Sype

Wolters Kluwer

Published by:
Kluwer Law International B.V.
PO Box 316
2400 AH Alphen aan den Rijn
The Netherlands
E-mail: lrs-sales@wolterskluwer.com
Website: www.wolterskluwer.com/en/solutions/kluwerlawinternational

Sold and distributed by:
Wolters Kluwer Legal & Regulatory U.S.
920 Links Avenue
Landisville, PA 17538
United States of America
E-mail: customer.service@wolterskluwer.com

ISBN 978-94-035-3506-7

e-Book: ISBN 978-94-035-3966-9
web-PDF: ISBN 978-94-035-3976-8

The Authors

Michael Birnhack is a Professor of Law at the Buchmann Faculty of Law, Tel Aviv University (TAU). His research focuses on information technology law, and in particular, privacy and data protection law. His 2010 book *Private Space* (in Hebrew) won the Annual Book Prize of the Israeli Political Science Association. His recent book *Constitutional Privacy* (in Hebrew) was published in 2023. Prof. Birnhack has co-edited a special volume of Theoretical Inquiries in Law on privacy, with Prof. Julie Cohen and Prof. Mireille Hildebrandt. He has also edited a volume on privacy in Hebrew, published in *Law, Society and Culture*. He has published numerous articles and book chapters on privacy, on issues of the cooperation between government and private companies in surveillance, secondary use of medical data for research purposes, CCTVs in schools, digital remains, as well as theoretical studies. He has won numerous research grants, from the Israel Science Foundation, the Ministry of Science, the Israeli Internet Society, and was part of a European Union (EU) consortium under the seventh research program, and a PhD network under Horizon 2020.

Prof. Birnhack served on the Schoffman Committee that has reviewed Israel's data protection law (2007); he served as a sub-contractor to the EU, in its examination of Israel's adequacy status in 2008–2010. He was a three-time member of the Public Council for the Protection of Privacy, appointed by Ministers of Justice. He was also a member of the Israeli Democracy's Institute initiative for a new privacy law, and is an ethics expert of the EU.

At TAU, he served as Associate Dean (Research) from 2017 to 2021; he founded and directed the S. Horowitz Institute for Intellectual Property (2015–2021), directed the Parasol International LLM Program (2015–2020), and founded the Privacy Clinic (2022). He is a member of the University's Privacy Committee.

The Authors

Omri Rachum-Twaig is a Technology, Cyber, and IP Partner at FISCHER, an Adjunct Professor of Law at the Buchmann Faculty of Law, TAU, and a senior fellow at the President Shamgar Center for Digital Law and Innovation at TAU. His practice and research focus on the intersection of law and technology, including intellectual property, privacy and data protection, artificial intelligence, and cyber and information technology.

After clerking for Supreme Court Justice Yoram Danziger, he earned his PhD (Law) in Intellectual Property, focusing on copyright law doctrine and theory. He regularly publishes scholarship in the fields of copyright, artificial intelligence, computer law, and cyberspace in leading academic journals worldwide. His first book *Copyright Law and Derivative Works: Regulating Creativity* was published with Routledge Press.

Dr Rachum-Twaig won several prizes and grants including the Volkswagen Foundation grant, the Wolf Foundation Prize for Young Academics, and the Cegla Prize for Young Scholars. He also teaches several classes at the Buchmann Faculty of Law and the Coller School of Management and is a Certified Information Systems Security Professional.

Table of Contents

Table of Contents

List of Abbreviations

AA	Administrative Appeal
AC	Administrative Case
ACH	Additional Civil Hearing
ACrH	Additional Criminal Hearing
ACRI	Association for Civil Rights in Israel
BoI	Bank of Israel
CA	Civil Appeal
CC	Civil Case
Class A.	Class Action
Crim. A.	Criminal Appeal
Crim. C.	Criminal Case
CSB	Central Statistics Bureau
DPO	Data Protection Officer
ECHR	European Convention of Human Rights
EU	European Union
FATCA	Foreign Account Tax Compliance Act [US]
FATF	Financial Action Task Force
FCt	Family Court
FOIA	Freedom of Information Act
FTA	Free Trade Agreement
GDA	Genetic Data Act
GDP	Gross Domestic Product
GDPR	General Data Protection Regulation [EU]
HCJ	High Court of Justice
HMO	Health Maintenance Organization
ICCPR	International Covenant on Civil and Political Rights
IDF	Israel Defence Forces
ILITA	Israeli Law, Information and Technology Authority
ISA	Israel Security Authority
LA	Labour Appeal

List of Abbreviations

LC	Labour Case
LCA	Leave for Civil Appeal
LCrA	Leave for Criminal Appeal
LDA	Labour Dispute Appeal
LFA	Leave to Family Appeal
MCP	Miscellaneous Civil Petition
MCrP	Miscellaneous Criminal Petition
MoE	Ministry of Education
MP	Miscellaneous Petition
NII	National Insurance of Israel
NIS	New Israeli Shekel
OECD	Organisation for Economic Co-operation and Development
OM	Opening Motion
PA	Palestinian Authority
PD	*Piskey Din* (Official publication of Supreme Court cases)
PDA	Prohibition of Defamation Act
PLO	Palestine Liberation Organization
PP Authority	Privacy Protection Authority
PPA	Privacy Protection Act, 1981
SC	Small Claims
TAU	Tel Aviv University
UK	United Kingdom
UN	United Nations
US	Unites States
WTO	World Trade Organization

Note to Readers

Translations of legislation, case law, and other sources from Hebrew are by the authors, with the following exceptions: for the Basic Law: Human Dignity and Liberty, we used the Knesset's official translation (https://m.knesset.gov.il/EN/activity/documents/BasicLawsPDF/BasicLawLiberty.pdf). For the Privacy Protection Act, 1981, we used an unofficial translation by the Ministry of Justice (https://www.gov.il/BlobFolder/legalinfo/legislation/en/ProtectionofPrivacyLaw57411981unofficialtranslatio.pdf).

In citing the dates of Israeli law, we used only the Gregorian calendar and omitted the Jewish year. We refer to legislation as 'Act' rather than 'Law', and reserve the latter term for more general reference to the law.

We translated names of public agencies and corporations into English and transliterated private names in English.

Cases published in the official Israeli publication (*Piskey Din* – PD) are cited accordingly; yet unpublished cases are searchable according to their number, on the Courts' website (https://supreme.court.gov.il/Pages/HomePage.aspx) or commercial publishers.

Note to Readers

General Introduction

§1. Geography

1. Israel lies on the eastern shores of the Mediterranean Sea. It comprises a land area of 22,072 square kilometres, including East Jerusalem and the Golan Heights.[1] Israel borders Lebanon in the north, Syria in the northeast, Jordan in the east, and Egypt in the south. There are peace accords with Egypt (as of 1979), and Jordan (1994).

2. East Jerusalem was annexed to Israel in 1967, at the end of the Six Day War.[2] It comprises a land area of 126 square kilometres.[3] The Golan Heights were annexed in 1981,[4] and comprise a land area of 1,153 square kilometres.[5]

3. Israel also controls most of the West Bank, which in total comprises a land area of 5,860 square kilometres.[6] Per the 1993 Oslo Agreement (as supplemented in 1995, by the second Oslo Agreement), with the Palestine Liberation Organization (PLO), the area is divided into three kinds: Area A is under the administrative and police control of the Palestinian Authority (PA); Area B is under the PA's administrative control, but security is shared between Israel and the PA; Area C is administered by Israel alone.[7]

4. As of 2005, Israel does not occupy the Gaza Strip.

5. This book refers to the law in Israel (including East Jerusalem and the Golan Heights), excluding the West Bank, although we will be referring to the privacy rights of Israeli, Jewish settlers and of Palestinians who live there.[8]

---

1. Israeli Central Bureau of Statistics (CBS), Area of Districts, Sub-Districts, Natural Regions and Lakes, 72 Statistical Yearbook for Israel, Table 1.1 (2021), at https://www.cbs.gov.il [Hebrew].
2. *See* Government and Judicial Procedures Order (No. 1), 1967.
3. Jerusalem Institute for Policy Research, https://jerusaleminstitute.org.il/blog/%D7%92%D7%93%D7%95%D7%9C%D7%94-%D7%91%D7%A9%D7%98%D7%97/ [Hebrew].
4. Golan Heights Act, 1981.
5. CBS, Table 1.1, *supra* n. 1.
6. CIA, West Bank, The World Factbook (2022), https://www.cia.gov/the-world-factbook/countries/west-bank/#geography.
7. Israeli-Palestinian Interim Agreement on the West Bank and the Gaza Strip, Isr.-PLO, 28 Sep. 1995.
8. *See* Part II, Ch. 2.

§2. Population

6. As of August 2022, Israel's population is 9.56 million people.[9] This figure includes 354,000 people who live in East Jerusalem,[10] and 52,500 people who live in the Golan Heights.[11] The population in the West Bank is estimated to be 3 million people, of whom 2,568,000 (85.6%) are Palestinians, and 432,000 (14.4%) are Israeli settlers.[12]

7. The composition of the Israeli population is the following (latest data is from 2020): 6,873,900 (74%) are Jewish, 1,671,300 (18%) are Muslim, 179,500 (2%) are Christian, 146,800 (1.6%) are Druze, and the remainder 416,700 (4.4%) are classified without a religious affiliation.[13]

8. Israel's population is relatively young: 3,263,900 (36%) are below the age of 20.[14]

9. The most populous city is the capital, Jerusalem, with 966,209 people. Tel Aviv is the second largest city, with 467,875 people; however, the central metropolitan area, covering 14 municipalities, comprises 1,481,356 people. Population density is 433 people per square kilometre.[15]

§3. Political System

10. Israel is a parliamentary democracy. The President is the head of state, but this is mostly a ceremonial office and the President lacks formal political power.[16] The Prime Minister is the head of the executive branch, namely the government. The legislature, the Knesset, is composed of 120 elected members.

11. Elections are national (i.e., they are conducted in one geographical unit) and representative.[17] The result is that the Knesset is comprised of several parties, and

9. CBS, Population, *The Statistical Monthly for Israel*, Table 1 (August 2022), at https://www.cbs.gov.il/he/publications/doclib/2022/yarhon0822/b1.pdf.
10. M. Korach & M. Hoshen, *Data about Jerusalem – Existing Situation and Trends of Change* 20 (The Jerusalem Institute for Policy Research 2021).
11. CBS, Population by District, Sub-District and Religion, 72 *Statistical Abstract of Israel 2021*, Table 2.15, at https://www.cbs.gov.il/he/publications/doclib/2021/2.shnatonpopulation/st02_15x.pdf.
12. CIA, West Bank, The World Factbook (2022), https://www.cia.gov/the-world-factbook/countries/west-bank.
13. CBS, Population, by Population Group, Religion, Age, Sex and Number of Males per 1,000 Females, 72 *Statistical Abstract of Israel 2021*, Table 2.5, at https://www.cbs.gov.il/he/publications/doclib/2021/2.shnatonpopulation/st02_05x.pdf.
14. CBS, Population, by Population Group, Religion and Sex, 72 *Statistical Abstract of Israel 2021*, Table 2.3, at https://www.cbs.gov.il/he/publications/doclib/2021/2.shnatonpopulation/st02_03.pdf.
15. The World Bank, Population Density (People per sq. km of land area) – Israel (2021), https://data.worldbank.org/indicator/EN.POP.DNST?locations=IL.
16. Basic Law: The President of the State, Art. 11.
17. Basic Law: The Knesset, Art. 4.

a government, having to win the Knesset's vote of trust, is a coalition government. This structure also means that the Knesset is relatively weak vis-à-vis the government.

12. Political parties should be registered and are autonomous in their activities. There are several grounds that may lead to disqualify registration: If the party's goals and actions, explicitly or implicitly, call for the denial of the existence of the State of Israel as a Jewish and democratic state; contain incitement to racism; support military campaign of an enemy state or terrorist organization against Israel, or if there is a reasonable basis to assume that the party will serve as a cover for illegal actions.[18]

§4. The Judiciary

13. Israel's judiciary comprises a third branch of government. It is independent, and judges are expected to rule only according to the law.[19] Judges are appointed by the President, according to recommendations of a nine-member committee, chaired by the Minister of Justice: Three members are Supreme Court justices, two are government ministers, two are appointed by the Knesset, and two are representatives of the Israeli Bar Association.[20] To appoint a Supreme Court Justice, a majority of seven members is required. Judges serve on the bench until the age of 70.[21]

14. The main Israeli judicial system comprises three instances: Twenty-nine Magistrate courts, six District courts – which serve both as courts of appeals on Magistrate courts, and have exclusive jurisdiction over civil matters which exceed the sum of NIS 2.5 million (approximately USD 758,000), and serious crimes.[22] The District Courts have administrative divisions, where judges are individually appointed to handle certain matters such as building and zoning laws, as well as economic divisions, tasked with specific powers. The Supreme Court is the highest court in the state, composed of fifteen Justices. It hears appeals over District courts' decisions, and has discretion whether to hear appeals on appeals. The Supreme Court has exclusive jurisdiction for petitions directed against the government (unless the administrative division of the District Court is specifically authorized to handle such issues), and against legislation. In the latter mode, the Court operates as the High Court of Justice (HCJ).[23]

15. Alongside the civil system, there is a labour court system, comprising of five regional labour courts, and a National Labour Court, which serves as a court of appeals, and has some jurisdiction in few enumerated matters, such as collective

18. Basic Law: The Knesset, Art. 7A; Parties Act, 1992, s. 5.
19. Basic Law: The Judiciary, Art. 2.
20. *Ibid.*, Art. 4.
21. Courts Act [Consolidated Version], 1984, ss 7(c)(2), 13.
22. *Ibid.*, s. 51.
23. Basic Law: The Judiciary, Art. 15.

agreements.[24] In some cases, the HCJ hears petitions over the National Labour Court's decisions, which is discretionary.[25]

16. Family law is adjudicated by designated Magistrate Courts, but religious courts (Jewish Rabbinical courts, Muslim Shari'a courts, and several courts of Christian congregations) have exclusive jurisdiction over matters of status, namely marriage and divorce.[26] The HCJ on occasion hears petitions against religious courts' decisions.[27]

§5. Legal System

17. Israel does not have a Constitution, but does have several Basic Laws that have a constitutional status. Some of these Basic Laws address structural elements (Basic Law: The President of the State; Basic Law: The Government; Basic Law: The Knesset; Basic Law: The Judiciary; Basic Law: State Comptroller). The Basic Law: Jerusalem anchors Jerusalem as Israel's capital, and the Basic Law: Israel – The Nation State of the Jewish People, determines the name, flag, state emblem, anthem, determines Hebrew as the language of the state and Arabic as enjoying a 'special status', and various other national elements.

18. Two more Basic Laws, both enacted in 1992, anchor particular human rights as fundamental rights. The Basic Law: Freedom of Occupation declares the right to engage in any occupation, profession, or trade. The Basic Law: Human Dignity and Liberty contains protection for the following rights: Preservation of life, body, and dignity (Article 2); personal property (Article 3); protection of life, body, and dignity (Article 4); personal liberty (Article 5); departure and entry into the country (Article 6); and privacy (Article 7).

19. The rights are not absolute and a general limitation clause (Article 8) allows for the infringement of such rights, if some conditions are met: 'One is not to violate the rights accorded by this Basic Law save by means of a law that corresponds to the values of the State of Israel, which serves an appropriate purpose, and to an extent that does not exceed what is required, or on the basis of a law, as aforementioned, by force of an explicit authorization therein.' Under these two Basic Laws, the Supreme Court has assumed the role of judicial review,[28] and may declare Knesset laws unconstitutional. Since 1992, the Court applied this power in twenty instances, regarding laws or sections in laws.[29]

---

24. Labour Courts Act, 1969, ss 24–25; Labour Courts Decree (Establishment of Regional Courts), 1969.
25. *See, e.g.*, HCJ 4111/19 *Doe v. National Labour Court* (2019).
26. Family Court Act, 1995, ss 2–3; Palestine Order in Council, 1922, Arts 47, 51.
27. *See, e.g.*, HCJ 2679/22 *Doe v. The High Rabbinical Court in Jerusalem* (2022).
28. *See* CA 6821/93 *United Mizrahi Bank Ltd. v. Migdal Cooperative Village*, 49(4) PD 221 (1995).
29. *See* A. Fuchs, *How Many Laws Have Been Voided until Today by the High Court of Justice?* (Israel Democracy Institute 2020), at https://www.idi.org.il/articles/22273 [Hebrew].

20. Israeli law is mostly a Common Law system, which is the heritage of the British Mandate to Palestine (1922–1948). In practice, this means that courts routinely interpret legislation, and where needed, develop the law. Courts also apply the principle of binding precedent.

§6. Economy

21. Israel's economy is one of free market, with some regulated areas. The World Bank classifies Israel as a high-income economy.[30]

22. Israel is a member of the Organisation for Economic Co-operation and Development (OECD) since 2010; a member of the World Trade Organization (WTO) since 1995, and has Free Trade Agreements (FTAs) with the United States (1985), the EU (2010), and several other countries.

23. The Gross Domestic Product (GDP) for 2021 was USD 481.6 billion, and the GDP per capita was USD 51,430.[31] The growth rate for 2021 was 8.2%.[32] At present, unemployment is low, with 4.3%. The national debt at 2021 was NIS 1,006,579 million.[33]

24. The annual budget for 2021 was NIS 609,143,215,000.[34] The main spendings are education NIS 67.38 billion (11%), national insurance NIS 65.14 billion (10.7%), military NIS 62.21 billion (10.2%), health NIS 55.31 billion (9.08%).[35]

25. Leading economic sectors that contribute to the GDP (updated to 2020) are financial services, real estate, scientific and technical administrative support (17.75%), information and communication (12%), education (6.8%), health (6.55%), local administration, defence, and national security (5.92%), arts and entertainment (2.7%).[36]

26. The main trading partners in 2020 were the EU (29.24%), the United States (26.2%), China (8.45%), and the United Kingdom (7.4%).[37]

---

30. The World Bank, Israel (2021), https://data.worldbank.org/indicator/EN.POP.DNST?locations=IL.
31. *Ibid.*
32. *Ibid.*
33. CBS, Government Sector, 72 *Statistical Yearbook for Israel* 2021, Table 25.5, at https://www.cbs.gov.il/he/publications/doclib/2021/25.shnatongeneralgovernmentsector/st25_05.pdf.
34. Accountant General, *The State Budget for the Fiscal Year 2020–2021*, Main Points of the Budget and Multi-Year Budget Plans (30 Aug. 2021), at https://www.gov.il/blobFolder/policy/state-budget-main-2021-2022/he/state-budget_2021-2022_state-budget-main-2021-2022-file.pdf.
35. *Ibid.*, at 15.
36. CBS, National Accounts, 72 *Statistical Yearbook for Israel* 2021, Gross Domestic Product (GDP) of Total Economy, by Industry, Table 11.3, at https://www.cbs.gov.il/he/publications/doclib/2021/11.shnatonnationalaccounts/st11_03x.pdf.
37. CBS, Exports, by Industry and Main Country of Destination, 72 *Statistical Yearbook for Israel 2021*, Table 13.12, at https://www.cbs.gov.il/he/publications/doclib/2021/13.shnatonimportsandexpo

27. The High-Tech industry plays a central role in the Israeli economy. In 2021, it grew by more than 10% and was estimated at approximately NIS 237 billion, comprising 15.3% of the Israeli GDP.[38] The total of Israel's High-Tech sector exports stands at 54% of all Israeli exports, and is evaluated at approximately USD 67 billion.[39] Among the OECD countries, Israel leads in the investment in research and development of its GDP, which stands at 5.4% (in 2020), but governmental investment is only 9.6% (in 2021), the lowest among OECD countries.[40] Israel was ranked fifteenth in the Global Innovation Index in 2021, down from its best rank (tenth) in 2019.

28. The number of employees in the Israeli High-Tech industry was about 362,000 people (in 2020), which makes up 10% of the Israeli workforce, the highest rate in the world. About 800 start-ups raised about USD 27 billion in 2021.[41]

29. The fields of activity in the High-Tech economy are diverse. The prominent are development of corporate software (25%), fintech (17%), cyber security (13.7%), and the remainder developing products for online commerce, communication, content and media, smart transportation, health, and food tech.[42]

§7. Social Values

30. Israeli society is saturated with fundamental tensions. The ongoing Israeli–Palestinian conflict, the continuing occupation of the West Bank and the Jewish settlements are sources for external and internal tensions. Externally, Israel has unsteady borders with Lebanon and Syria, and ongoing unrest with the Hamas government in Gaza. Internally, the political issues result in Jewish–Arab conflicts, occasionally with some riots (2000, 2021).

31. Another source of tension within the Jewish society is the place of religion. Israel declares itself to be a Jewish state, with no separation between state and religion. Some segments of the population – the Haredi, ultra-Orthodox Jewish segment, openly call for the installation of Jewish law as the law of the country, whereas other segments call for full separation of state and religion. In practice, the tensions result in debates about personal status, LGBT rights, burial practices, transportation on Shabbat, regulation of Kosher food, and more.

---

rtsofgoodsandservices/st13_12x.pdf; CBS, Imports and Exports of Business Services, by Country, Table 13.16, at https://www.cbs.gov.il/he/publications/doclib/2021/13.shnatonimportsandexportsofgoodsandservices/st13_16.pdf.

38. Israel Innovation Authority, Israeli High-Tech (2022) [Hebrew], at https://innovationisrael.org.il/InnovationReport2022.
39. *Ibid.*
40. *Ibid.*
41. *Ibid.*
42. *Ibid.*

32. As of 2019, Israeli is undergoing a continuous political crisis, with five election cycles within three years. The former Prime Minister is at present on trial for various corruption charges, but is still a member of the Knesset and leads his party. Over the years, we have witnessed growing polarization within the Israeli society.[43]

43. O. Kenig & A. Shapira, *Israel as Election Leader*, Israel Democracy Institute (2022), at https://www.idi.org.il/articles/39226 [Hebrew].

Part I. Privacy Protection in Israel

Chapter 1. Privacy Protection in the Constitution

§1. Introduction

33. Israel does not have one unified Constitution, but a series of Basic Laws, which have constitutional status. These Basic Laws enjoy the highest legal status in Israeli law, and may serve as a basis for the courts to declare a law, regulation, or an executive policy to be unconstitutional and thus void.[44]

34. Public authorities are also subject to administrative law, namely principles and rules developed over the years by the courts. These rules apply mostly to the decision-making process, such as which considerations should not be taken into account, procedural rights such as due process, and some substantial elements, requiring decisions to be reasonable and if the decisions involve balancing of rights and public interests, to be proportional.[45]

§2. The Basic Law

35. The Basic Law: Human Dignity and Liberty, enacted by the Knesset in March 1992, reads, in Article 7, as follows:

(a) Every person has the right to privacy and to intimacy in his life.
(b) There shall be no entry into the private premises of a person, without his permission.
(c) No search shall be held on the private premises of a person, upon his body, in his body, or among his private effects.
(d) The confidentiality of a conversation of a person, his writings or his records shall not be violated.

44. For the status of the Basic Laws, *see*, *e.g.*, B. Medina, *Human Rights Law in Israel* (Sacher Press 2016) [Hebrew].
45. For Israeli administrative law, *see* D. Barak-Erez, *Administrative Law* (Nevo 2010–2017) [Hebrew].

36. Accordingly, privacy enjoys an explicit constitutional status in Israeli law.[46] However, the Basic Law does not define privacy or other terms mentioned in this article, such as 'intimacy', and it remains for courts to interpret the scope of the right. Article 7(a) protects privacy in a broad, general manner, and is not limited to the three specific situations listed in Articles 7(b)–7(d). The particular situations require further interpretation, for example, what does consent mean in the context of entering into one's private premises (Article 7(b)), or whether communication data is included in 'conversation', mentioned in Article 7(d).

37. Constitutional privacy means that all government branches are obliged to respect privacy. The government's policies and Knesset legislation should not violate privacy, with the exception prescribed in the Basic Law itself. Per Article 10, the Basic Law has had a prospective application, thus immunizing all laws that predated it. However, the Supreme Court clarified that post-1992 amendments to pre-1992 laws were subject to constitutional review.[47] Pre-1992 legislation, while its validity cannot be challenged, is to be interpreted and applied in line with the Basic Law.[48] In some cases, constitutional privacy may also bind non-public entities, such as private bodies deemed under Israeli law to be 'hybrid' bodies, due to their monopoly over the provision of vital services, such as the electricity company or burial companies, or due to the fact that they are funded by the government.[49]

38. The constitutional right to privacy applies to living people within Israel, and binds the state within its territory. However, the constitutional obligations may be carried to the West Bank, via doctrines of administrative law and international human rights law.[50]

39. Privacy, like other rights enumerated in the Basic Law, is subject to a general limitation clause. Article 8 reads: 'One is not to violate the rights accorded by this Basic Law save by means of a law that corresponds to the values of the State of Israel, which serves an appropriate purpose, and to an extent that does not exceed what is required, or on the basis of a law, as aforementioned, by force of an explicit authorization therein.' This clause resembles the limitation clause in Article 8(2) of the European Convention of Human Rights (ECHR), as well as Article 52 of the EU Charter on Fundamental Human Rights. Article 8 enables the balancing of privacy with other human rights, or with public interests, such as national security, law enforcement, public health, or similar considerations.

---

46. *See* HCJ 8070/98 *ACRI v. Ministry of Interior*, 58(4) PD 842 (2004). For discussion, *see* M. Birnhack, *Constitutional Privacy in Israeli Law*, in *Oxford Handbook on the Israeli Constitution* (A. Barak, B. Medina & Y. Roznai eds, Oxford U. Press, forthcoming 2023); M. Birnhack, *Constitutional Privacy* (Bar-Ilan & Nevo Press 2023) [Hebrew].
47. CA 6821/93 *United Mizrahi Bank Ltd. v. Migdal Cooperative Village*, 49(4) PD 221, 308, 652–653 (1995).
48. ACrH 2316/95 *Ganimat v. State of Israel*, 49(4) PD 589 (1995).
49. HCJ 731/86 *MicroDaf v. Israel Electric Corp. Ltd*, 41(2) PD 449 (1987); CA 294/91 *Jerusalem Burial Society v. Kestenbaum*, 46(2) PD 464 (1992).
50. *See* discussion in Part II, Ch. 2, below.

40. Article 8 was interpreted in numerous constitutional cases to include several conditions: First, to permit the infringement of constitutional privacy (or other enumerated rights), the infringing act should be explicitly authorized by a Knesset Act. Indirect authorization would typically be insufficient. The extent to which the authorization should be explicit may vary, depending on the kind of harm.[51] Second, the law at stake should aim at an 'appropriate purpose'. Third, the law at stake should befit the values of the State of Israel. Article 1A declares these values to be 'the values of the State of Israel as a Jewish and democratic state'. Fourth, the infringing Act should be proportional.[52] Courts developed the proportionality requirement to include three sub-tests. First, the means undertaken to achieve the legitimate purpose should fit the purpose in a general manner (the 'fit test'); second, the law at stake should have chosen the least harmful means to achieve the purpose ('least harmful means' test), and third, a detailed evaluation of the added benefit to the legitimate purpose, compared to the added harm caused by the particular measure undertaken (the 'narrow proportionality test').[53]

§3. Judicial Interpretation

41. The Supreme Court has explained the importance of privacy in its constitutional context in several cases. In *Dayan v. Vilk*, decided two years after the enactment of the Basic Law, the Court reviewed a police decision to prohibit a demonstration outside the house of a prominent rabbinical figure, who was also involved at the time in guiding a political party.[54] The Court framed the case as a conflict between the privacy of the rabbi, considered to be a public figure and his neighbours' privacy on the one hand, and the freedom of demonstration, conceptualized as freedom of expression, on the other hand. Justice Aharon Barak instructed: 'Now, once [privacy] deserved a legislated constitutional status, it should be interpreted broadly, … not technically; with generosity, … in a substantive manner, rather than a legalistic one.'[55] Barak explained the importance of privacy: 'The right to privacy draws the line between the individual and the public, between the "self" and the society. It draws a space where the individual is let alone to develop his "self" without others' interference.'[56] The Court reviewed the police's balancing of the competing rights, concluding that privacy and freedom of expression are to be balanced horizontally, namely, the rights at stake were considered to be of similar weight. The solution resorted to 'time, place, and manner' rules, directing the police to permit the demonstration, although in a nearby public square, rather than immediately outside the rabbi's home.

51. HCJ 10203/03 *HaMmifkad HaLeumi Ltd. v. Attorney General*, 62(4) PD 715, 821–824 (2008).
52. For elaboration, *see* A. Barak, *Proportionality in Law* (Nevo 2010) [Hebrew].
53. For a thorough discussion, *see* A. Barak, *Proportionality and Principled Balancing*, 4(1) L. & Ethics Hum. Rts. 1 (2010).
54. HCJ 2481/93 *Dayan v. Vilk*, 48(2) PD 456 (1994).
55. *Ibid.*, at 470, internal citations omitted.
56. *Ibid.*, at 471.

42. In an appeal on the conviction of private investigators who entered homes under a pretext and took intimate photos to serve as evidence in divorce cases, Justice Hanoch Ariel commented that:

> The right to privacy is, *inter alia*, a derivative of the right to dignity. Recognising privacy is recognising man as an autonomous individual, entitled to singularity vis-à-vis others. This singularity enables the person to fortress in his personality as having a meaning and worthy of respect. A human being's privacy is his dignity and property, too. This is the framework in which he may, if he so chooses, develop his selfhood and determine the level of interference of society in his behaviour and privacy actions. This is his proprietary, personal and mental 'fortress'.
>
> This right is one of the fundamental human rights in Israel. It is one of the liberties that shape the Israeli regime as democratic and it is one of the fundamental rights that establish dignity and liberty that a person deserves qua being a person.[57]

43. These statements were repeated numerous times in subsequent cases.

44. The Constitutional dimension of privacy played a central role in an important data-related case. At stake in *ACRI v. Ministry of Interior* were data transfers from the national population registry (managed within the Ministry of Interior) to various public authorities, such as the Israeli Broadcasting Authority, and to (private) banks.[58] Justice Dalia Dorner, in the majority opinion, commenced with a bold statement: 'The right to privacy in Israel is a fundamental right.'[59] She ruled that data transfers to the banks failed to meet the first condition set in the Basic Law's limitation clause: There was no statutory authorization permitting such transfers.[60] As for the data transfers to public bodies, Dorner ruled that these were not limited to the minimum needed to achieve specific goals, and that the number of people authorized to access the data on the receiving end was not specified.[61] Accordingly, these data transfers failed the proportionality test. Justice Asher Grunis, in a dissenting opinion, offered his view of constitutional privacy: That the right to be let alone was not confined to the home, and that there was a 'concern for the state's excess power that might concentrate substantial data about citizens and residents and misuse the data'.[62] He joined the majority regarding data transfers to public authorities, but considered the transfer to banks to be *de minimis*, since customers already identify themselves to the bank teller, and the additional data received from the population registry was meant to authenticate their identity. Following this case, the Knesset amended the law, to facilitate such transfers, subject to various limitations.[63]

---

57. Crim. A. 5026/97 *Gal'am v. State of Israel*, 9 (1999).
58. HCJ 8070/98 *ACRI v. Ministry of Interior*, 58(4) PD 842 (2004).
59. *Ibid.*, at 846.
60. *Ibid.*, at 853–855.
61. *Ibid.*, at 852.
62. *Ibid.*, at 856.
63. Population Registry Act (Amendment No. 11), 2007.

45. Subsequent cases applied the Basic Law directly. In several cases, the Supreme Court ordered the government to discontinue various practices, as they failed to meet the first condition set out in the limitations clause, that of statutory authorization. In *Manna v. Tax Authority*, the Court found that a joint police-tax roadblock operation was unconstitutional.[64] The police set supposedly routine roadblocks in East Jerusalem, to check drivers' license. When a driver was pulled over, a police officer asked for the driving license, handed the data over to a tax collector who then checked online whether the driver owed any taxes. If there were such debts, the driver was required to pay on the spot, or the car was impounded. The Court found that the police was not authorized to transfer the data to the tax collectors.

46. Similarly, the Court reviewed another police practice, of officers demanding citizens to present an identification document even without concrete suspicion, and then check the data online in police databases. The Court found that the police had the authority to demand the presentation of an identification document, but not to undertake additional data processing.[65] In yet another case, the Court found that the Ministry of Defence lacked 'clear, detailed, and explicit' authorization' to conduct covert surveillance of a former officer, who claimed welfare payments.[66] Justice Daphne Barak-Erez succinctly explained, that 'need is not a source of authorization.'[67]

47. Direct constitutional review of legislation based on privacy grounds is rare. The Court found that the Criminal Procedure Act (Enforcement Powers – Communications Data), 2007 was constitutional, as it contained sufficient detailed instructions as to how and when law enforcement agencies can collect communication data (as opposed to the contents of communications).[68] The Court added some interpretive guidelines: A court can issue a communications data search order only when a particular suspect and a particular suspicion have been determined. Police general intelligence was prohibited.[69] This interpretation, the Court held, rendered the Act proportional.

48. The COVID-19 pandemic raised core privacy issues. Following the outbreak of the pandemic in Israel in early 2020, the Government used various emergency powers to order the Israel Security Authority (ISA, a.k.a. Shin Bet) to apply its security-oriented technological capabilities for the purpose of contact tracing. The ISA tool is based on location data presumably received from cellular phone providers. In the first ruling, the Court focused on the question of authorization, and allowed the mass surveillance to continue for a short period, until the government

64. HCJ 6824/07 *Manna v. Tax Authority*, 64(2) PD 479 (2010).
65. HCJ 4455/19 *Tebeka Advocacy for Equality & Justice for Ethiopian Israelis v. Israel Police* (2021), rehearing denied, HCJFH 2707/21 *Israel Police v. Tebeka Advocacy for Equality & Justice for Ethiopian Israelis* (2021).
66. LCA 2558/16 *Doe v. Ministry of Defence*, para. 39 (2017).
67. *Ibid.*, at paras 58–66.
68. HCJ 3809/08 *ACRI v. Israel Police* (2012).
69. *Ibid.*, at para. 16.

initiated authorizing legislation.[70] Chief Justice Esther Hayut commented that the ISA operation was particularly harmful to privacy, due to the security-related nature of the ISA, and the involuntary and covert collection of data. The Knesset then enacted a temporary Act for six months (which was then extended by six more months due to an election cycle), that authorized the surveillance. In a second case, a majority of the seven-justice panel confirmed the constitutionality of the new Act, but found that the government failed to properly operationalize it.[71] Responding to the Omicron variant, the government reinstated surveillance for five days. The Supreme Court approved the emergency measure.[72] These cases illustrate that the Court was concerned with privacy violations, but also that it tends to defer to the Knesset on such matters, and is more likely to interfere with unauthorized governmental actions.[73]

49. Overall, the Supreme Court's constitutional privacy jurisprudence is inconsistent, and is yet to adopt a coherent understanding of privacy. The Court does not always clearly articulate the harm to privacy, and often assumes that there is such a harm and continues to examine the proportionality of the measure undertaken. The Court often reduces the harm to be the exposure of personal data (as in the Omicron case), or to potential data leakage, overlooking additional privacy harms.[74] The Court's constitutional privacy jurisprudence is subject to additional critique, regarding its framing of constitutional conflicts as 'horizontal' or 'vertical', a framing that affects the level of judicial scrutiny.[75]

§4. Decisional Privacy

50. Israeli law has not included decisional privacy under the heading of constitutional privacy, unlike American law (at least until 2022). Issues such as a woman's right to terminate pregnancy or same-sex relationships are framed as a matter of human dignity and autonomy, rather than privacy. Nevertheless, there are few judicial comments, all as *obiter dicta*, echoing the American approach, in the context of parenthood.[76]

---

70. HCJ 2109/20 *Ben-Meir v. Prime Minister* (2020).
71. HCJ 6732/20 *ACRI v. The Knesset* (2021).
72. HCJ 8196/21 *ACRI v. The Government (2021).*
73. For critique of these cases, *see* M. Birnhack, *Privacy in Crisis: Constitutional Engineering and Privacy Engineering*, 24 L. & Govt in Israel 149 (2022) [Hebrew]; S.A. Duke, *Nontargets: Understanding the Apathy Towards the Israeli Security Agency's COVID-19 Surveillance*, 19(1) Surveillance & Soc'y 114 (2021).
74. HCJ 1946/17 *Zeidan v. The Government* (2022), in which the Court dismissed petitions challenging the constitutionality of the Biometrics Act.
75. Birnhack, *Constitutional Privacy*, *supra* n. 46.
76. *See, e.g.*, LFA 5082/05 *Attorney General v. Doe*, 60(3) PD 201, 220 (2005) (a mother's right not to disclose the identity of her child's father when handing the child for adoption); LFA 1118/14 *Doe v. Ministry of Social Affairs* (2015) (a woman's wish to be a parent is a constitutional right, derived, *inter alia*, from privacy).

§5. STATUTORY DUTIES

51. In addition to constitutional privacy, the Privacy Protection Act, 1981 (PPA) applies to the State, per section 24, and with specific arrangements for data transfers between public bodies and private entities (PPA, Chapter D). Part II elaborates on the PPA.

Chapter 2. National Application of Regional and International Conventions

§1. Introduction

52. Israel is a member of numerous international conventions, some of which refer also to privacy in a general matter, such as the International Covenant on Civil and Political Rights (ICCPR), 1966, and the International Covenant on Economic, Social and Cultural Rights, 1966, or in a concrete context, such as the United Nations Convention on the Rights of the Child, 1989.

§2. Israel and European Data Protection Law

53. The EU considers Israel as a 'third country' which is not bound by the EU's directives and regulations or the EU Court of Justice jurisprudence.

54. In 2011, the EU recognized Israel as having an adequate data protection law, under Directive 95/46/EC.[77] The adequacy recognition was limited to automated transfers and processing,[78] and applied to the 'State of Israel, as defined in accordance with international law.'[79] This means that the adequacy status does not refer to the West Bank, nor does it refer to East Jerusalem or the Golan Heights, which the EU does not consider part of Israel. At present, under the General Data Protection Regulation (GDPR), the adequacy status is reassessed.[80]

55. Israel is not a member of the Council of Europe, and hence is not bound by the ECHR and the European Court of Human Rights. Israeli courts rarely refer to the ECHR.[81] Israel has not signed or ratified Convention 108[82] but has the status of an observer country.

---

77. Commission Decision of 31 Jan. 2011 pursuant to Directive 95/46/EC of the European Parliament and of the Council on the adequate protection of personal data by the State of Israel with regard to automated processing of personal data.
78. *Ibid.*, at Art. 1 (and *see also* recital 12).
79. *Ibid.*, at Art. 2(2) (the decision 'is without prejudice to the status of the Golan Heights, the Gaza Strip and the West Bank, including East Jerusalem, under the terms of international law'). *See also* recital 14.
80. GDPR, Art. 45(9).
81. *See, e.g.*, in the context of privacy, HCJ 7052/03 *Adalah Legal Center for Arab Minority Rights in Israel v. Minister of the Interior*, 61(2) PD 202, 326–327 (2006). Israeli courts tend to refer mostly to American, Canadian, and British sources, in this order of frequency. *See* S. Navot, *Israel: Creating a Constitution – The Use of Foreign Precedents by the Supreme Court (1994–2010)*, in *The Use of Foreign Precedents by Constitutional Judges* 129 (T. Groppi & M. Ponthoreau eds, Hart Publishing 2013).
82. European Convention for the Protection of Individuals with Regard to Automatic Processing of Personal Data.

§3. OTHER TREATIES

56. Israel is a member of the Budapest Convention on Cyber Crime, which it had joined in 2016. Israel is also a member of the Financial Action Task Force (FATF) as of 2018, which deals with anti-money laundering activities.

Chapter 3. Privacy in Electronic Communications

§1. INTRODUCTION

57. Article 7(d) of the Basic Law: Human Dignity and Liberty states that 'The confidentiality of conversation of a person, his writings or his records shall not be violated.' This constitutional instruction applies directly to the state and its organs, other public bodies, and 'hybrid bodies', and may affect the interpretation of rights in private law as well.

58. The PPA includes a designated provision pertaining to privacy in electronic communications and, as explained below, generally applies to the collection and processing of personal data in electronic forms.[83] Israeli law has not adopted specific legislation for the use of cookies and other online tracking technologies.

59. However, there is peripheral legislation that addresses certain aspects of privacy in the context of electronic communications. One example is the Communications Act (Telecommunication and Broadcasting), 1982 ('Telecom Act') that adopted anti-spam provisions. Another example is the Wiretapping Act, 1979, which provides for certain criminal and civil restrictions over interception of communications. Additional relevant laws are the Criminal Procedure Act (Enforcement Powers – Communications Data), 2007 and the Computer Act, 1995.

§2. ANTI-SPAM

60. Section 30A of the Telecom Act includes a robust anti-spam framework. It generally applies to 'Marketing Messages', which are defined as one of the following: (i) a message distributed commercially for the purpose of encouraging the acquisition of a product or service or to spend money in any other method; (ii) a message distributed to the public with the purpose of propaganda or donation request; (iii) a message distributed to the public and includes an offer to call a certain phone number for the purpose of receiving a certain message. The definition also captures 'Automated Dialling System' which are telecommunication facilities serving for automatic dialling or routing of a sequence of calls to a group of recipients for the purpose of relaying a recorded message. However, this framework does not cover un-automated phone calls, or physical mail.

61. Marketing Messages conveyed via Automated Dialling Systems, fax, SMS/MMS or retrievable electronic messages generally require an explicit opt-in consent, which should be provided in written form or by a recorded call (section 30A(b)). In addition, Marketing Messages should follow certain formalities: Marketing Messages relayed over electronic mail should include the word 'Ad' in their

83. *See* discussion in Part II, Ch. 2.

subject line, and if relayed over SMS/MMS, at the beginning of the Marketing Message (section 30A(e)(1)(A)). The Marketing Message must include the name, address, and contact details of the advertiser, the right of the recipient to opt-out at any time with a simple means to provide such opt-out request (section 30A(e)(1)(B)). Courts differ on whether an opt-out link would be sufficient to satisfy this requirement, or if other opt-out communication channels such as email or phone calls should be mandatory.[84]

62. Israeli courts considered Marketing Messages relayed over private social media inboxes to be subject to the requirements set forth above.[85] This is also true to specific 'private messaging accounts' provided to users of certain services and apps. However, targeted marketing ads appearing on social media, including posts and other elements, are not considered Marketing Messages.

63. There are certain exceptions to the opt-in requirement under section 30A(b). First, donation requests and political parties' messages are exempt from the opt-in consent requirement with respect to Marketing Messages, provided that the recipient did not inform the sender, in advance, that it declines receipt of such messages (section 30A(b1)).[86]

64. Second, telecommunications service providers acting as mere conduits are exempt from liability for Marketing Messages.[87]

65. Third, in business-to-business contexts, a business is allowed to send one initial Marketing Message to another business to solicit the interest of such other business in its products and services without opt-in consent, provided that the mandatory notices and opt-out requirements apply. Any further Marketing Message is subject to opt-in consent.

66. Fourth, section 30A(c) allows sending Marketing Messages to existing or potential customers who purchased or negotiated the purchase of products or services of a business, without their opt-in consent, provided that the following conditions are met: (i) a notice is sent to such customers after their inquiry with the business explaining that such Marketing Messages will be sent in the future, (ii) that such notice allows consumer an opportunity to opt-out from future Marketing Messages, and (iii) that the Marketing Messages are confined to the same type of products or services the customers purchased or negotiated. With respect to condition (i), the Supreme Court ruled that such notice could be sent at any time after the purchase or negotiation, provided that it occurs before first sending a Marketing

84. CA 4704/20 *Ben Ami v. Facebook Ireland Ltd*, paras 22–24 (2021).
85. SC (Tel Aviv) 32611-12-15 *Radziner v. Cellcom Israel Ltd.* (2016). The issue has not yet been decided by the Supreme Court. For discussion, *see* CA 3599/18 *Shapira v. Ofri* (2018).
86. *See, e.g.*, Class A. (Tel Aviv, District) 3468-09-14 *Roded v. D.B.S. Satellite Services (1998) Ltd.*, paras 35–39 (2019).
87. *See* definition of 'Advertiser', under s. 30A(a), which excludes sending Marketing Messages by licensed telecommunication providers.

Message to the customer.[88] Courts have not yet fully established how such notices should be provided to customers, but most courts have ruled that reference to general terms and conditions was insufficient.[89]

67. The Telecom Act provides for criminal and civil sanction for violations of the Marketing Message requirements. From a criminal perspective, violations may incur a fine of up to NIS 226,000 (and up to NIS 75,300 for office holders and directors). From a civil perspective, violations can trigger statutory damages of up to NIS 1,000 per message for personal claims. Indeed, there are numerous such lawsuits.[90] In addition, violations are eligible for class action litigation, where non-monetary damages could be claimed if proven.[91]

§3. Wiretapping

68. The Wiretapping Act, 1979 is the main legislation that governs the interception of communications in Israel. The Act distinguishes between covert interception, namely the interception of a conversation without the consent of any party thereto, which is prohibited, and monitoring and recording of a conversation with the consent of one of the parties thereto, which is permitted. Specific provisions set the conditions for lawful wiretapping by law enforcement and security agencies. The Wiretapping Act itself only includes criminal sanctions. Violations of the Wiretapping Act constitute infringement of privacy as per section 2(2) of the PPA.

69. A party to the conversation is defined in section 1 of the Act as: '(1) the speaker, (2) the person to whom the conversation is addressed, (3) the person who transmits telecommunications, or (4) to whom the transmission is addressed'. Accordingly, if one party to the conversation has recorded it, even without the other party's consent, this recording is lawful.[92]

70. A 'conversation' is defined in the Act to include any method of transmission of telecommunication, including computer communications, and therefore the applicability of the covert interception provisions is broad.[93] However, the types of content or signals that may constitute a 'conversation' are left undefined. The case law

88. CA 534/17 *Lapid v. Cellcom Israel Ltd.* (2019).
89. Class A. (Tel Aviv, District) 16620-09-19 *Ben Porat v. 'Lelo-Hafsaka' Radio Ltd.*, para. 33 (2020).
90. For rulings in lawsuits regarding violations of the Marketing Message requirements, *see* https://www.isoc.org.il/freedom-of-internet/spam/spam-verdicts (The Israeli Internet Association; in Hebrew).
91. *See, e.g.*, Class A. (Haifa, District) 57094-10-19 *Raveh v. S. Shastowitz Ltd.* (2020) (The court approved a class action, while acknowledging compensation for non-monetary damage. The court noted the justifications for class action where the proven damage was too low to manage separate claims, at para. 113).
92. *See* the definition of 'covert interception' in s. 1 of the Act. *See also* Crim. A. 1497/92 *State of Israel v. Zubberi* 47(4) PD 177, 197 (1993). Within the public service, there is a prohibition against recording, even if the recorder is a party to the conversation. *See* Civil Service Regulations, ss 43.91–43.92 (June 2022).
93. *See* definition of 'call' in s. 1 to the Act.

on the matter is not necessarily clear as to which types of information are subject to the Act,[94] but there is a general understanding that it applies to all information communicated in transit during a conversation (as opposed to information stored at-rest by any party to the conversation).[95]

71. Covert interception of conversations without lawful authorization, the use of content obtained using unlawful covert interception, and installing equipment intended to allow unlawful covert interception are criminally prohibited under the Wiretapping Act with penalties of up to five years of imprisonment.[96]

72. The Wiretapping Act also provides for instances where covert interceptions are lawful, when official permits have been granted. Generally, covert interceptions are lawful for law enforcement agencies and national security purposes if an interception permit is obtained from the President of a District Court or their deputy (for law enforcement purposes) or the Defence Minister (for national security purposes). The requesting entity must show that the wiretapping is required for one of the above-mentioned purposes and that such purpose is not outweighed by the expected violation of privacy. The Act also authorizes conducting covert interceptions without such permits in urgent circumstances (sections 5 and 7). In such cases, the head of the law enforcement agency (for law enforcement purposes) or the Prime Minister (for national security purposes) may permit interception without a court order for a period not exceeding 48 hours (sections 5(a) and 7(a)). The agencies under this Act are the Israeli Police, the ISA, and the Intelligence Division in the Israel Defence Forces (IDF).[97]

73. To support covert interception capabilities of law enforcement agencies, the Telecom Act (section 13) authorizes the Prime Minster to require licensed telecommunications providers to maintain interception capabilities and allows access to such capabilities to agencies upon obtaining permits under the Wiretapping Act.[98]

74. The Wiretapping Act explicitly prohibits using evidence obtained through unlawful covert interceptions, with the exception of proceedings related to serious crimes and under special circumstances (section 13). This is a more stringent approach than the respective provisions of the PPA (section 32).[99]

---

94. For example, in the context of a 'conversation' conducted by e-mail, *see* Crim. C. (Tel Aviv, District) 40206/05 *State of Israel v. Philosoph*, para. 8(a)(4) (2007).
95. *See* O. Rachum-Twaig, *Computerized Searches*, Tel Aviv Law Review Forum (2022) [Hebrew].
96. *See*, *e.g.*, CC (Tel Aviv, Magistrate) 23637-09-10 *State of Israel v. Pridan* (2011) (A private investigator with previous convictions for similar offenses was sentenced to eighteen months of probation, of which six months of community service and a fine of NIS 30,000); CC (Rehovot, Magistrate) 56840-11-12 *State of Israel v. Bennita* (2014) (Wiretapping during divorce proceedings; the infringer was sentenced to six months of probation and a fine of NIS 3,500).
97. *See also* discussion in Part X, Ch. 3.
98. *See also* discussion in Part X, Ch. 4.
99. *See*, *e.g.*, Crim. A. 1302/92 *State of Israel v. Nahemias*, 49(3) PD 309 (1995).

75. In the context of covert interception of conversations conducted over instant messaging services over the internet, there has been debate whether the Wiretapping Act applies, or whether other acts applicable to searching computer content are more suitable. Search and interception powers of law enforcement agencies are divided between the Wiretapping Act and the Criminal Procedure Ordinance [Arrest and Search], 1969 (Search Ordinance). Section 23A of the Search Ordinance includes designated provisions pertaining to search in computers and computer content and sets forth that no such search will be conducted without a search warrant issued by a Magistrate Court judge. The explanatory notes of the Wiretapping Act and the Search Ordinance clarified that while the former focuses on interception of data in transit, the latter focuses on data at rest. Courts have reiterated this distinction.[100]

76. In the case of messaging services, end-to-end encryption is commonly employed, which renders the interception of the conversation in-transit unintelligible. Thus, law enforcement agencies have used technologies aiming at intercepting the conversation in clear text in the device's storage. Whether such interceptions are subject to the Wiretapping Act or the Search Ordinance affects the manner in which permits and search orders should be obtained, as well as doctrines regarding the applicability of evidence obtained unlawfully.

77. An inquiry committee headed by the Deputy Attorney General found that the Police has used covert technologies that bypass end-to-end encryption, and at times exceeded the wiretapping warrants by recording data which was not 'conversation', such as contacts lists, personal notes, and the list of applications on a device, as well as accessing data from a time prior to the order.[101] The committee found that the excessive data was not used. The committee further concluded that the use of the spying technology was authorized under the Wiretapping Act, under section 10A, which allows entry into physical places in order to execute a wiretapping order. The committee found this to apply also to remote electronic access. This legal construction is controversial.[102]

§4. Communication Data for Law Enforcement

78. The Criminal Procedure Act (Enforcement Powers – Communications Data), 2007 provides for a special arrangement allowing law enforcement agencies, subject to a warrant from a competent court, to obtain communications data from communications service providers licensed under the Telecom Act, all for the purpose of saving lives, preventing or investigating crimes or criminals, or confiscating property under law (section 3(a)).

---

100. *Philosoph*, *supra* n. 94.

101. *See* Ministry of Justice, Report of the Inquiry of Eavesdropping Communications Between Computers Team (2022).

102. *See*, *e.g.*, M. Birnhack, 'From Urich to Pegasus: On Constitutional Privacy in Police Investigations', ICON-S-IL Blog (2022) [Hebrew]; Rachum-Twaig, *supra* n. 95.

79. The types of data available under the Act are limited to three categories and generally exclude the content of conversations within such communications. First, they include location data which is defined as the location signal of the end-equipment. Second, they include subscription data defined as identification data of the subscriber to the communications, the type of service subscribed for, and payment methods. Third, they include transport data defined as the type of communications, the recipient end equipment and identity, and the time, duration, and bandwidth of the communication.

§5. Computers Act

80. The Computers Act, 1995 was enacted to criminalize various actions made in connection with computers of 'computer content' defined as either software or data. The prohibitions of the Act generally follow the data security principles of confidentiality, integrity, and availability, and thus render it illegal to interfere with the proper functioning of computers (section 2(1)), affecting the integrity of computers and computer content, including deleting, altering, or causing the output of the data to be false (sections 2(2) and 3) or compromising the confidentiality of computer content by unlawfully accessing it (section 4). The Telecom Act also criminalizes the development of software intended to commit any of the foregoing computer crimes, infringe privacy or allow wiretapping (section 6).[103]

103. *See, e.g.*, Crim. C. (Tel Aviv, District) 40061/06 *State of Israel v. HaEfrati* (2006).

Chapter 4. Other Relevant National Legal Provisions Regarding the Protection of Privacy

§1. Introduction

81. The main privacy legislation, other than the constitutional anchor in the Basic Law: Human Dignity and Liberty,[104] is the PPA.[105] Note that the PPA contains privacy torts, data protection regulations, and some regulation of governmental data transfers. Chapter 3 discussed privacy in electronic communications. This chapter outlines additional layers of privacy protection in Israeli legislation. This chapter addresses health data, genetic data, biometric data, financial data, and educational data. This is not an exhaustive legislative inventory of privacy-related rights and duties, and there are additional, specific references in numerous legislation. The PPA governs all kinds of data collection and processing, unless a specific law explicitly overrules it. All legislation is subject to the Basic Law, either directly, or as an interpretive guideline, for pre-1992 legislation.[106]

§2. Health Data

82. The main legislation in this area is the Patients' Rights Act, 1996.[107] The Act contains a general duty for medical staff to respect patients' privacy (section 10(a)) and requires the directors of medical institutions to issue instructions in this regard (section 10(b)). The Act sets a duty of confidentiality which applies to the medical staff (section 19(a)), and a duty imposed on the general director of medical institutions to assure that employees abide by this duty of confidentiality (section 19(b)). The Act allows for the transfer of medical data in certain cases: with the patient's consent, when there is a legal duty to hand over data, for continuity of the medical treatment, for protecting another person's health or the public health (subject to a hearing by an ethics committee), or for professional publications, as long as the patient's identifying details do not contain identifying data (section 20). Specific legislation imposes a duty of confidentiality on psychologists, regarding their patients, with some exceptions.[108]

83. The People's Health Ordinance, 1940, legislated by the British Mandate of Palestine and absorbed into Israeli law in 1948, requires a person who suffers from a contagious disease and their doctor to notify the Ministry of Health of this condition (section 12) as soon as possible. The Minister of Health can declare a certain disease as contagious for this purpose (section 20). This power was used during the

104. *See* Part I, Ch. 1.
105. *See* Part II.
106. *See* Part I, Ch. 1.
107. For extensive discussion, *see* A. Carmi, 1 *Health and Law* 846–847, 870–873, 1654–1656 (M.S. Wattad ed., Nevo 2d ed. 2013) [Hebrew].
108. Psychologists Act, 1977, s. 7.

COVID pandemic. Additional powers were put in place, authorizing epidemiological inquirers to demand infected people to hand over certain information, for the purpose of tracing contacts (section 20H).

84. Rules issued by the Ministry of Health regulate the use of health data for the purpose of research.[109] Such data are held mostly by the four Health Maintenance Organizations (HMOs). The rules permit secondary use of health data for research purposes. The rules prioritize using such data with the subject's consent, and in the absence of consent, instructs to use only data that had been anonymized prior to the secondary use. Transfer of data from an HMO to a third party is subject to prior approval of a Helsinki committee. Additional rules set some requirements for data transfers.[110]

§3. Genetic Data

85. The Genetic Data Act, 2000 (GDA) contains detailed regulation of genetic tests and genetic consulting. The Act requires informed consent for DNA sampling (section 11(a)), and when the sampling is meant for research, the consent should also be in writing (sections 11(b), 23(2)), but exempts research that utilizes non-identifying DNA samples or de-identified samples, if there is no possible way to re-identify the subjects (section 13).[111]

86. The GDA clarifies that the PPA governs the processing of genetic data, unless the GDA instructs otherwise (section 17).

87. The GDA reiterates a duty of confidentiality (section 18), refers to the Patients' Rights Act for rules regarding data transfers (section 19), and permits transfer of genetic information to a relative of the subject, unless the subject has objected (section 20). Such objection may be overruled by an Ethics Board (section 20). The Act further prohibits an employer to require an employee or a candidate for employment to reveal genetic data (section 29(a)), with limited exceptions for specific workplaces, as determined by the Minister of Health (section 29(d)).[112]

88. Security agencies, such as the Israeli Defence Forces (IDF) may conduct genetic tests and use the data for specific purposes, including criminal investigations, intelligence for national security purposes, identifying bodies, and related research (section 32(a)). Such a database is subject to the PPA (section 35).

---

109. Director General, Ministry of Health, Circular 1/2018, Secondary Uses of Health Data (2018), https://www.health.gov.il/hozer/MK01_2018.pdf.
110. Director General, Ministry of Health, Circular 2/2018, Collaborations Based on Secondary Uses of Health Data (17 Jan. 2018), https://www.health.gov.il/hozer/MK02_2018.pdf.
111. For discussion, *see generally*, Carmi, *supra* n. 109, 1335–1345 [Hebrew]; C. Shalev, *Genetic Databases: Private and Public in Research and Development*, 27 Medicine & L. 70 (2002) [Hebrew].
112. For privacy in the labour context, *see* Part IX, Ch. 4.

§4. BIOMETRIC DATA

89. Biometric data for formal identification purposes is regulated in a specific law: The Inclusion of Biometric Identifiers and Biometric Data in Identification Documents and a Database, 2009 ('Biometric Data Act'). The Act orders the collection of certain biometric data from residents for the purpose of including them in the national identity card and passports (section 3(a)). ID cards are issued to citizens above 16 years old, and passports and issued to any citizen who requests it. The data are also stored in a central database (section 3(c)). The biometric data are facial features, and with the explicit consent of the subject, also finger scans (section 3(c1)). The incentive to provide finger scans was that the official documents have a longer duration – ten years for those who submit both kinds of biometric data, five years for those who declined to provide finger scans (section 5A), although the Minister of Interior has the power to extend the duration, a power which has been utilized. The Act contains detailed arrangements for the transfer of such data to security bodies and law enforcement agencies (sections 16–22). The Act contains duties of confidentiality (sections 23–24), and data security (section 25). The Act requires the appointment of a Data Protection Officer (DPO) (section 26), and establishes various regulatory bodies for oversight.

90. The Biometric Data Act was received with scepticism and public criticism,[113] as well as legal criticism, aimed in particular at the central database.[114] The critique resulted in an initial pilot period (which was concluded), changes to the kinds of data collected, and various official reports of oversight bodies. Several petitions were submitted to the Supreme Court, challenging the Act's constitutionality. However, the Court declined, for the time being, to discuss the cases, framing the harm to privacy as a potential leak, and accordingly, concluded that the petitions were premature.[115]

91. Biometric data also plays a role in certain doctrines under the PPA. It is explicitly defined in the Privacy Protection Regulations (Data Security), 2017 as a factor for determining the security level of databases,[116] and was considered by the National Labour Court as highly sensitive type of personal data affording heightened rights to employee data subject.[117]

---

113. *See* K. Nahon, *The Politics of the Biometric Database*, 2 L. Soc'y & Culture 271 (2019) [Hebrew]; A. Marciano, *Israel's Biometric Project in Mainstream Israeli Press*, 2 L. Soc'y & Culture 237 (2019) [Hebrew].
114. *See* O. Tene, *Israel's Biometric Database Law: Risks and Opportunities*, 17 Hamishpat 421 (2012) [Hebrew].
115. HCJ 1947/17 *Zeidan v. Israeli Government* (2022).
116. *See* Part V, Ch. 4 below.
117. *See* Part IX, Ch. 4 below.

§5. Financial Data

92. Banks and similar financial institutions are under the obligation to keep data confidential. The duty is not anchored in any specific legislation, but rather in the general duty of contractual confidentiality and in case law.[118] Breaching a duty of confidentiality regarding a person's private affairs is a violation of privacy under sections 2(7)–2(8) of the PPA. There are several exceptions to the duty of confidentiality, meant to assure compliance with local and some foreign tax laws, as well as anti-money laundering law.

93. Banks are required to collect certain data in order to identify the account holder's country of residency for tax purposes.[119] Data about foreign residents may be transferred to a foreign country, according to a data exchange agreement, based on the OECD's Automatic Exchange of Financial Account Information in Tax Matters,[120] and specifically, in the case of American citizens, according to an Israel–US 2014 Agreement to implement the American law on the matter, the Foreign Account Tax Compliance Act (FATCA). The Israeli Supreme Court reviewed the Israeli legislation that facilitated the data transfer, and upheld it.[121]

94. Licensed operators of exchange businesses are required to report any transaction that exceeds the amount of NIS 50,000.[122]

95. Employees of the Tax Authority are subject to a duty of confidentiality.[123]

96. As of April 2019, financial data is gathered in a centralized, systematic, and large scale system, according to the Credit Data Act, 2016.[124] This Act replaced a 2002 Act, which allowed for some data collection and processing. The 2016 Act expanded this operation dramatically. Under the Act, the Bank of Israel (BoI) is authorized to collect credit data, hold them in a database, and share the data with credit data companies and customers (section 3). The purpose of the Act is to increase competition in the local credit market, make the market more accessible, and create an unidentified resource for the BoI (sections 1(a), 16, 44). The financial data at stake include information about financial obligations, their payment or non-payment, requests for loans, information about financial accounts that include elements of loans and credit (section 2). The sources of the data are the Administrator General, the Enforcement Authority, BoI, courts, banks, the Electricity Company, and credit services (section 19). The Act contains detailed arrangements as to the

118. *See* I. Amit, *Evidentiary Privileges and Protected Interests: Discovery Proceedings in Civil and Criminal Law* 985–994 (Nevo 2021).
119. Income Tax Ordinance [New Version], ss 135D–135H.
120. *See* https://www.oecd.org/tax/exchange-of-tax-information/automaticexchange.htm.
121. HCJ 8886/15 *Republicans from Abroad in Israel v. Government of Israel* (2018), confirming the constitutionality of Income Tax Ordinance [New Version] (Amendment No. 227) and various regulations to implement it.
122. Income Tax Ordinance [New Version], s. 141A.
123. Income Tax Ordinance [New Version], s. 231.
124. *See also* Part X, Ch. 5.

various agents in this field, as well as some specific privacy-related rules, e.g., the BoI is required to appoint a DPO (section 18) – one of the few statutory such positions. A customer may request that financial data shall not be used to prepare a credit report about them (section 30).

97. The Financial Information Services Act, 2021, which entered into force in June 2022, regulates such services.[125] A service provider may collect and process financial information from a closed list of sources, and only for the purpose of providing services to the client (section 25). The data may be collected and the service granted only after the service providers provides a clear and concise explanation about the service, and after a written contract is signed (section 26). The service provider may retain the data only for as long as the service is needed, and in any case, for no longer than three years (section 27(a)), thereafter the data should be deleted (section 27(b)).

§6. Educational Data

98. Several scattered rules pertain to students' privacy, albeit in specific contexts. The Pupils Rights Act, 2000 (section 14) imposes a duty of confidentiality on recipients of pupils' personal data, who are permitted to use it only for executing their official roles.

99. A series of binding guidelines issued by the General Director of the Ministry of Education (MoE) contain various limitations on data transfers. For example, rules about conducting research at schools;[126] recommendations about using digital devices;[127] and guideline regarding CCTVs in schools.[128]

100. The Students' Rights Act, 2007 limits the use of personal data provided by candidates to higher education institutions: The recipient institution should not use the data for a purpose other than for the registration process, or with the student's consent.

125. *See also ibid.*
126. Director General, Ministry of Education, No. 0281, Rules Pertaining to Research in the Educational System (2022), at https://apps.education.gov.il/mankal/horaa.aspx?siduri=378 [Hebrew].
127. Director General, Ministry of Education, No. 0100 Students' Use of Devices for Studying (2016), at https://apps.education.gov.il/mankal/horaa.aspx?siduri=31#_Toc256000028 [Hebrew].
128. Director General, Ministry of Education, No. 0119 CCTV in Schools: Introduction and Installation (2015), at https://apps.education.gov.il/mankal/horaa.aspx?siduri=134 [Hebrew], and discussion in Part X, Ch. 5.

Part II. National Data Protection Law

Chapter 1. Background: General Description of National Data Protection Law

§1. Introduction

101. The PPA comprises the core of Israel's data protection law. The PPA addresses both traditional privacy torts and data protection issues, specific regulation of governmental data transfers, within and outside the executive branch, as well as the specific issue of direct marketing.[129] Although the PPA separates privacy torts and data protection, there are some overlaps, both in the underlying factual situations and in the legal rules. Thus, one factual scenario may give rise to more than one legal scheme.

102. The PPA's layers are the result of several expert committees in the late 1970s and early 1980s. There were some amendments over the years, notably in 1996 and 2007. However, since 2007, there has been legislative stagnation. Attempts to amend the PPA were few and so far, unsuccessful. The Ministers of Justice issued various regulations handling specific issues over the years, most are relatively technical, but some, such as the 2017 Privacy Protection (Data Security) Regulations, 2017 ('DataSec Regulations'), which came into force in May 2018, contain substantive duties.

103. The data protection regime is European in spirit, both in the underlying understanding of privacy as a derivative of human dignity, and in the more concrete framing of privacy as control.[130] EU law has influenced some courts, especially the National Labour Court and some district courts, in their privacy jurisprudence. In 2011, the EU recognized Israel as having an adequate data protection legal regime, a recognition that is currently reassessed under the GDPR.[131] Israeli law has various other foreign influences, especially from American law.

---

129. Bulk mailing, i.e., spam, is regulated separately, in the Communications Act (Telecommunication and Broadcasting), 1982. *See* discussion in Part I, Ch. 3.

130. *See, e.g.*, HCJ 6824/07 *Manaa v. Israel Tax Authority*, 64(2) PD 479 (2010), paras 34–39.

131. For Israel's adequacy status, *see* Part I, Ch. 2.

104. Israeli data protection law should be read on the background of the constitutional status of privacy in Israel.[132] Constitutional privacy applies directly to the state and governmental authorities, to some private entities that perform public or semi-public functions, and has also been applied by courts in the context of labour law. Constitutional privacy may affect the interpretation of the law also in the private realm, especially in cases where there is a conflict between privacy and another human right, such as freedom of expression.[133]

105. This chapter outlines the background of Israeli data protection law, its overall structure, and key themes. Chapter 2 in this Part discusses the scope of the law, and Chapter 3 presents its key concepts and definitions, elaborated also in subsequent parts.

§2. Background and Development

106. In 1974, the Ministry of Justice appointed an expert committee, with the task of proposing a privacy law.[134] The committee was chaired by Justice Yitzhak Kahan, later the Chief Justice of the Supreme Court. Other members included prominent legal figures, such as Professor Aharon Barak (later, Chief Justice), constitutional scholars, and Dr Ruth Gavison, who was then writing her doctoral dissertation at Yale Law School, and has become a prominent privacy scholar. The Kahan Report was published in 1976. It examined the UN Universal Declaration of Human Rights, and the law in the US, UK, Germany, France, and Canada. Its recommendations were the basis of Chapters A and C of the PPA, enacted in 1981. The report dealt with traditional privacy, namely interactions between people, typically based on a single encounter, and not necessarily informational privacy. These torts included harassment, photography in certain circumstances, appropriation of a person's name or image, breach of confidentiality, and publication of private information. These are all privacy torts, listed in sections 2 and 2A of the PPA. Chapter C contains some defences and exemptions.

107. During its deliberations, the Kahan committee decided to exclude issues of informational privacy – later known as data protection. Another committee was formed, chaired by Knesset Member and Chair of the Knesset Constitution and Law Committee, David Glass.[135] The Glass Report addressed concerns raised by the increase of databases. It referred to the law in Sweden, the US, France, and Luxemburg. The recommendations served as the basis for Chapter B of the PPA, which deals with data protection issues. In 1996, Amendment No. 4 updated this chapter,

132. *See* Part I, Ch. 1.
133. *See, e.g.*, CA 8954/11 *Doe v. Doe*, 66(3) 691, 761–768 (2014).
134. Committee for the Protection of Violation of Intimacy (Y. Kahan, Chair, Jerusalem 1976).
135. Committee for Prevention of Harm to Citizens by Computerized Databases (D. Glass, Chair, Jerusalem 1981).

and added regulation of direct mailing. Another substantial amendment took place in 2007, via Amendment No. 9, which clarified the definition of consent, and added statutory damages for privacy torts.

108. Another committee was formed shortly after the PPA was enacted, chaired by a senior clerk at the Ministry of Justice, Haim Klugman, later the Director General of the Ministry, and the Chair of the Public Council for the Protection of Privacy.[136] The Klugman committee dealt with the transfer of governmental data, and its recommendations from 1982 formed the basis of Chapter D of the PPA in 1985.

109. Twenty years later, another committee was formed, chaired by then-Deputy Attorney General Joshua Schoffman, which reviewed the data protection regime.[137] The Schoffman report, submitted in early 2007, recommended various amendments, the gist of which were to ease some of the bureaucratic burden on data controllers by narrowing the database registration duty, enhancing data subjects' rights, and strengthening enforcement. Some of these recommendations served as the basis of proposals to amend the PPA fifteen years later, in the Privacy Protection Bill (Amendment No. 14).[138] To date, this bill has not yet been enacted.

§3. THE STRUCTURE OF THE PPA

110. The PPA reflects the committees' recommendations, but the lines between the various topics are not always clear-cut.

111. Chapter A of the PPA commences with a general principle – that 'No person shall infringe the privacy of another without his consent,' thus introducing the notion of consent, defined in section 3, to mean 'informed, express or implied consent'. The PPA does not define what privacy is; rather, section 2 lists twelve situations which are privacy violations. These are the privacy torts. Originally, the list contained eleven situations, but in 2011, the Knesset added, via Amendment No. 11, another tort, regarding the publication of a photograph of a person injured in a public place (section 2(4A)). The same amendment also added that the publication of a photograph of an identifiable body is a privacy violation, subject to some conditions (section 2A). Section 3 contains various definitions; section 4 classifies a privacy violation as a tort, and section 5 adds a criminal aspect to these violations. Section 6 reflects the *de minimis* principle, stating that there is no civil or criminal cause of action if the 'infringement [is] of no real significance.'

112. Importantly, while section 2 is phrased in a manner that may suggest that it contains a closed list of privacy torts, the Supreme Court clarified that this was not

136. Committee for Information Transfer between Public Bodies (H. Klugman Chair, Jerusalem 1982). For the Council, *see* Part VIII, Ch. 3.
137. Committee for Reviewing Legislation in the Area of Databases (J. Schoffman, Chair, Jerusalem 2007). One of the authors (Birnhack) was a member of the committee.
138. Privacy Protection Bill (Amendment No. 14), 2022.

the case. Alongside the statutory privacy torts, Chief Justice Barak wrote, Israeli common law continued to develop, especially in private law.[139] Based on this statement, the National Labour Court found that collecting biometric data – finger scans collected and used as an attendance registry in a public workplace without the employees' consent, was a privacy violation.[140] An administrative court (the District Court, under special authority) found that location data are also protected in certain circumstances.[141] A magistrate court found that retaining intimate photos of another person, taken with the person's initial consent which was then withdrawn, is a privacy violation.[142]

113. Chapter B of the PPA (sections 7–17I) contains a detailed data protection regime.[143]

114. Chapter C of the PPA (sections 18–22) contains some limitations to liability and defences, which refer to Chapter A – the privacy torts.

115. Chapter D of the PPA (sections 23–23G) addresses governmental data transfers. This chapter was based on the Klugman Report.

116. Chapter E of the PPA contains miscellaneous general instructions. Section 24 applies the PPA to the State – thus, a governmental act should meet both statutory and constitutional requirements. Section 25 allows for the continuation of a lawsuit submitted shortly before a person's death, or the submission of such a suit by family members within six months of death; section 26 sets the limitations for lawsuits to be two years – this is much shorter than the usual seven-year limitation in civil suits.[144] Chapter E contains also statutory damages (section 29A), which refer only to section 4, namely to privacy torts, rather than to data protection violations. Sections 30–31 refer to indirect liability of a publisher and distributer. Section 32 contains an exclusionary rule, by empowering a court to decide whether to allow or dismiss evidence which were obtained by violating privacy. The remaining sections deal with criminal and civil matters of data protection. Section 36 authorizes the Minister of Justice to issue related regulations.

117. The upshot of the above is that while data protection issues are dealt mostly within Chapter B of the PPA with some additional rules in Chapter E, some actions may also be subsumed under Chapter A. The classification may matter, for example in the case of statutory damages, which apply only to privacy torts, but not to data protection torts. The interaction between the statutory and constitutional dimensions are also important, when the agent at stake is the state or a state organ.

---

139. HCJ 6650/04 *Doe v. Regional Rabbinical Court, Netanya*, 61(1) PD 581 (2006).

140. LDA 7541-04-14 *New Histadrut (General Organization of Workers in Israel) v. Qalansawe Municipality* (2017).

141. AC (Tel Aviv, Admin. Court) 28857-06-17 *Caregiving Companies Association v. Ministry of Defence* (2019). An appeal overturned some of the findings, but not those relating to privacy.

142. Crim. C. (Krayot, Magistrate) 19692-07-21 *State of Israel v. Doe* (2022).

143. *See* Part II, Ch. 3.

144. Limitations Act, 1958, s. 5(1).

§4. Regulations

118. Under the Minister's Authority (section 36), several regulations have been issued over the years, setting procedures regarding the right to access personal data;[145] procedures for data transfer between governmental agencies;[146] adding security bodies that are exempt from access rights;[147] out of country data transfers;[148] and most recently, data security.[149] The Minister has also issued regulations regarding administrative fines under another Act.[150] Most of these regulations set procedures, but some have added substantial rights and duties, e.g., a duty to delete excessive data that is transferred between public bodies,[151] and data breach notification duties.[152]

§5. Administrative Regulations and Guidelines

119. The PPA establishes the position of a Database Registrar (section 12), to be appointed by the Government (section 7). The Registrar should meet statutory criteria to be eligible to be appointed as a Magistrate Judge.[153] The PPA lists various registration-related powers (sections 10(a)–10(b3), 10(f)), including the power to refuse registration,[154] and delete a registration. Note that managing and possessing a database that should be registered (section 8(c) sets the conditions) and that without registration, managing such a database is a criminal offense (sections 8(a) and 31A(a)(1)). The Registrar has the power and duty to supervise compliance with the PPA and related regulations (section 10(c)), and has powers to establish and manage an enforcement unit (sections 10(d)–10(e1)).

120. In 2006, the Ministry of Justice established a new unit, which integrated various authorities under the PPA as well as powers per the Electronic Signature Act, 2001 and the Credit Data Service Act, 2002 (which has since been repealed and

---

145. Privacy Protection Regulations (Conditions for Accessing Data and Procedures for Appeal on a Refusal to Allow Access), 1981.
146. Privacy Protection Regulations (Conditions for Retaining Data and Procedures for Data Transfers between Public Bodies), 1986.
147. Privacy Protection Regulations (Determining Databases that Contain Data not to be Revealed), 1987.
148. Privacy Protection Regulations (Transferring Data to Databases outside the Country), 2001.
149. Privacy Protection Regulations (Data Security), 2017.
150. Administrative Felonies Regulations (Administrative Fines – Privacy Protection), 2004, promulgated under the Administrative Felonies Act, 1996.
151. Privacy Protection Regulations (Conditions for Retaining Data and Procedures for Data Transfers between Public Bodies), 1986, s. 6, implementing PPA, s. 23E.
152. Privacy Protection Regulations (Data Security), 2017, s. 11(d).
153. Namely, a person with at least five years of experience as a lawyer. *See* Courts Act [Consolidated Version], s. 4.
154. *See, e.g.*, CA 439/88 *Database Registrar v. Ventura*, 48(3) PD 808 (1994), in which the Supreme Court clarified that the Registrar's discretion is limited to refusing the registration of illegal databases, including cases where the illegality is due to violating privacy rights. The Court approved a refusal to register a credit history database. A law regulating such activities was enacted only eight years later.

replaced with the Credit Data Act, 2016). The unit was initially called Israeli Law, Information and Technology Authority (ILITA), and was renamed as the Privacy Protection Authority in 2017 ('PP Authority').

121. The PP Authority has issued various instructions, guidelines, recommendations, and opinions over the years. While there is no explicit statutory authority for such regulations, an Administrative Court anchored this power in several PPA sections – section 10(c) that establishes the Registrar's power to supervise the compliance with the Act, the database registration powers, and the power to impose fines, as well as in a broad interpretation of the underlying purposes of the PPA.[155] The instructions are considered administrative guidelines, and reflect the general policies of the PP Authority and its interpretation of the PPA, but do not necessarily have independent binding power or preference over alternative interpretations in legal proceedings.[156] We address specific guidelines throughout the book, where pertinent.

§6. Additional Data Protection Legislation[157]

122. Another noteworthy legislation is the Class Actions Act, 2006. This Act regulates procedures regarding class actions, and permits such actions only if they fall within one of the cases mentioned in the Second Appendix to that Act. Privacy is not explicitly mentioned there. However, when defendant is a business, and there is a customer–business relationship, the situation falls within the first option in the Class Actions Act's appendix. When the facts of a case do not fit such a situation, courts refused to allow the class action to proceed. For example, when plaintiff submitted a class action against a municipality, the Court dismissed the case.[158]

123. Another Act worth mentioning is the Prohibition of Defamation Act, 1965 (PDA 1965). Both the PDA and the PPA deal with personal rights, and there are some cross-references in the PPA to the PDA. For example, the PPA, section 3 defines 'publication' by referring to the PDA; sections 18(1) and 18(2)(f), listing civil defences, references the PDA; section 27 applies various procedural rules from the PDA in the PPA context; sections 25 in both laws (continuation of a deceased's lawsuit) are similar, and rules about indirect liability (sections 30–31 in both laws) are almost identical. There are some differences, e.g., the PDA allows for a cause of action that occurred after a person's death under some conditions, whereas the PPA does not contain a similar option.

---

155. AC (Tel Aviv, Admin. Court) 24867-02-11 *IDI Insurance Co. Ltd. v. Database Registrar* (2012). An appeal was dismissed, with the Justice commenting that they agree with the decision. *See* AA 7043/12 *IDI Insurance Co. Ltd. v. Database Registrar* (2014).
156. ACH 7488/16 *Zeligman v. Phoenix Insurance* (2018), paras 62–67.
157. Part I, Ch. 4 above discussed additional legislation, containing specific privacy-related arrangements, regarding health data, genetic data, biometric data, financial data, and educational data. Some of these specific arrangements refer back to the PPA. Part I, Ch. 3, reviewed privacy in electronic communications.
158. CA 4110/18 *Doe v. Kadima Mada (Science Forward) Ltd.* (2019), para. 9.

§7. The Courts

124. With Israeli law being a common law system, courts have an important role in interpreting and developing the law. The above provided some examples, notably the judicial expansion of the legislative list of privacy torts. Additional examples are the interpretation of the term 'a person's private affairs', which appears several times in the PPA (sections 2(7), 2(8), 2(9)), with some extensions (section 23A).[159]

125. Courts have also interpreted key concepts such as the purpose limitation principle, discussed below.[160]

159. *See* Part II, Ch. 3 for elaboration.
160. Part III, Ch. 1.

Chapter 2. Scope of the National Law (Material, Personal, Territorial)

§1. INTRODUCTION

126. The main pillar of Israeli data protection law, Chapter B of the PPA applies to electronic databases, as defined under section 7 of the PPA. Other data-related activities may be subject to other chapters of the PPA. The PPA applies to living human beings (namely, in European parlance, 'natural persons'), rather than corporations or the dead, with a specific exception regarding some photographs; the PPA is territorial, and applies within the State of Israel, but may have some extra-territorial extensions in concrete contexts.

§2. MATERIAL SCOPE

127. The basic legal unit that underlies the PPA's data protection regime is that of a database, rather than personal data or the data subject. A database is defined as 'collection of data, kept by a magnetic or optic means and intended for computer processing' (section 7). This definition means that Chapter B does not apply to manual databases. Nevertheless, some non-automated processing of personal data is regulated under Chapter A of the PPA, which addresses privacy torts. For example, copying or using the contents of a letter, without the consent of the letter's author or its recipient, is an infringement of privacy (section 2(5)).

128. There are two exceptions to the definition of a database: One is for a personal, non-business collection of data; the second is a collection of data which includes only name, address or means of communication, without a characterization of the data (section 7). While the PPA does not contain a direct 'household activity' exemption (cf. GDPR, Article 2(2)(c)) these exclusions may in practice amount to such an exemption. Nevertheless, a household activity that violates another person's privacy may be considered a privacy tort under section 2.

129. The definition of a database refers to 'data', which contains both a content-based criterion and a subtle identification criterion.

130. As for the content-based criterion, section 7 of the PPA defines data (or 'information') as 'data on the personality, personal status, intimate affairs, state of health, economic position, vocational qualifications, opinions and beliefs of a person.' There is a further definition of 'sensitive data', which does not include 'personal status' and 'vocational qualifications', but adds the option for the Minister of Justice to determine 'sensitive data' by an Order. As of September 2022, no such Order has been issued.[161]

161. Section 2 of the PPA contains several references to the 'private affairs of a person', which was interpreted separately by the Court. *See* discussion in Part II, Ch. 3.

131. As for the identification-based criterion, the words 'of a person' were interpreted to refer to an identified person. In a case that dealt with the publication of architectural three-dimension imaging of the interior of a house, the Supreme Court found that if the home owner who commissioned the work can be identified via the imaging, then privacy rights apply.[162] The PP Authority also treats this definition as referring to identified or identifiable people, thus echoing the European definition of personal data (GDPR, Article 4(1)).[163] This means that the PPA does not apply to purely anonymous data. Newer legislation echoes the GDPR's identifiability criterion more clearly, such as the Credit Data Act, 2016.[164]

132. Unlike the GDPR, the PPA does not exclude national security activity or law enforcement activity (cf. GDPR, Articles 2(2)(b), 2(2)(d)). The PPA does apply to the state (section 24), but there are some exemptions for security bodies, such as less transparency for databases of security agencies (section 12(c)), exemptions from the right of access (section 13(e)(1)), and there are some limitations to the liability of security agencies and their employees (section 19). Other laws may override the PPA in order to facilitate national security interests.[165] In such a case, the balancing of the rival interests – privacy and national security – may be subject to a judicial review, under the rules pertaining to constitutional privacy.[166]

§3. Personal Scope

133. The PPA applies to living people. While the Interpretation Act, 1981 defines a 'person' to include also legal persons, namely corporations and a group of people, the PPA explicitly excludes corporations from most of its rules. Section 3 defines a person so not to include 'a body corporate' for the purposes of several, listed sections. These include section 7 – which defines 'data' and 'database'. Accordingly, corporations do not enjoy data protection rights. However, and as the Supreme Court clarified, a corporation is subject to duties to respect data protection rights.[167] The Knesset has rejected a proposal to recognize corporations' privacy.[168]

162. CA 1697/11 *Gottesman Architecture Ltd. v. Vardi* (2013).
163. *See* Database Registrar Guideline, 1-2010, Minimum Requirement for Identity Verification Processes of the Data Subject in Order to Provide Access to the Data about him in the Database (2010).
164. Credit Data Act, 2016, s. 2 defines 'identified data' to mean 'information that contains an identifying detail of a customer, or information that identifying details were removed therefrom, but with a reasonable effort it is possible to identify the person to whom the data pertains.'
165. For example, the Israeli Security Agency Act, 2002, which contains various authorizations to the agency, such as covert search (s. 10). *See also* discussion in Part X, Ch. 4, regarding national security agencies.
166. For constitutional privacy, *see* Part I, Ch. 1.
167. HCJ 648/99 *Nawie v. Knesset Speaker* (1999); CC (Haifa, Magistrate) 4901/08 *Graphonet Ltd. v. Peled* (2009).
168. Knesset Committee on Constitution and Law, Meeting No. 331 (16th Knesset, 22 Nov. 2004).

134. Few lower courts have commented that corporations may enjoy constitutional privacy rights.[169] The reasoning was that unlike the PPA, the Basic Law does not contain a definition of a 'person', and in other contexts, such as property, corporations have enjoyed constitutional rights.[170] Other courts have ruled against such recognition.[171] The Supreme Court addressed the issue in passing, in a freedom of information case. An attorney requested the National Insurance of Israel (NII) to hand over data about 2500 employers who may be entitled to refunds.[172] The NII refused, citing, *inter alia*, the privacy of the employers. The majority opinion mentioned in passing that corporations do not enjoy privacy, but Justice Issac Amit, in dissenting, opined that corporations should enjoy privacy in the context of freedom of information, pointing to a duty of confidentiality that the NII owes to tax payers, employers included.[173]

135. The view favouring corporate privacy has met scholarly criticism, explaining that the underlying normative principles and justifications of privacy do not apply to corporations, and that recognizing such rights would unjustifiably limit the public's access to vital information and evade various transparency duties.[174] Moreover, corporations enjoy various other rights, protecting their property, trade secrets, the integrity of their computerized systems, contractual confidentiality, e.g., in financial contexts, and more.

136. The PPA applies only to living people. While the PPA itself is silent about this matter, the Legal Capacity and Guardianship Act, 1962, which has a general application in Israeli law, states that 'A person has the capacity to rights and duties from the end of his birth to his death.' The Knesset has declined to extend privacy rights to the deceased.[175] Moreover, the PDA 1965, which protects a person's reputation and has many similarities to the PPA, diverges on this matter, and in section 5 allows the Attorney General to initiate criminal charges when a deceased person was defamed posthumously. No such rule applies to privacy.

137. The PPA does contain specific protections for the deceased. One is found in section 25, allowing family members to sue for the violation of the deceased's privacy which took place during their life, within six months of their death, as well as allowing a privacy lawsuit to continue after the plaintiff's death. Another specific protection for the deceased is a 2011 amendment which added section 2A to the

---

169. *See, e.g.*, CC (Haifa, District) 10434/96 *Keysarit Furniture Ltd. v. Ararat Insurance Ltd.* (2000).
170. *See, e.g.*, CA 6821/93 *Mizrahi Bank Ltd. v. Migdal Kfar Shitufi*, 49(4) PD 221 (1995).
171. *See, e.g.*, Crim. C. (Jerusalem, Magistrate) 102/05 *Mizrachi Bank Ltd. v. Shauli* (2005).
172. AA 7744/10 *National Insurance of Israel v. Mangal*, 66(1) PD 116 (2012).
173. *Ibid.*, at para. 16. Interestingly, in his book, Amit did not raise the question, described it as complicated, but did not offer any conclusive view. *See* I. Amit, *Evidentiary Privileges and Protected Interests: Discovery Proceedings in Civil and Criminal Law* 1136 (Nevo 2021) [Hebrew].
174. *See* M. Birnhack, *Private Space* 126–132 (Bar-Ilan & Nevo 2010) [Hebrew]; M. Birnhack, *Constitutional Privacy* (Bar-Ilan & Nevo 2022) [Hebrew].
175. Privacy Protection Act (Amendment No. 9) Bill, 2005; Knesset Committee on Constitution and Law, Meeting No. 214 (16th Knesset, 6 Jun. 2007).

PPA, determining that the publication of a photograph of an identified deceased person is a privacy violation, unless the person has consented to publication during their life, or that fifteen years have passed, or the immediate family has consented to the publication. This tort was added in response to press publications of photographs of bodies of people killed in terror attacks.[176]

138. Despite the legislative negation of posthumous privacy, the Supreme Court has ruled in one influential case that privacy rights persisted after death, and were operationalized by the person's heirs.[177] The case dealt with a financial dispute among the children of a deceased couple, from their prior relationships. The bank that managed the account at stake refused to hand over the data. The party that demanded access argued that the deceased no longer enjoyed privacy. The Court disagreed, explaining that this argument conflicts with the law's purpose. This view was criticized in the literature, first, because the legislation clearly does not award posthumous privacy rights; second, because the underlying justifications of the right to privacy do not support such a posthumous extension, and third, because this extension equates privacy with property, which raises numerous other difficulties.[178] The critique suggested narrowing the judicial comment to cases in which the data at stake refers to property: since the property itself – the bank accounts – passes over to the heirs, they have a right to access the data as the heirs, not because privacy is inheritable. Some lower courts adopted this critique.[179] But, when a psychologist refused to hand over her notes about the deceased to the deceased's family members, the district court agreed, explaining that privacy was a personal right.[180]

139. Israeli law does not at present regulate digital remains, namely personal digital data left after a user dies. This means that in practice, the Terms of Use offered by the online platforms dictate the fate of such digital remains, and who may have access thereto.[181]

§4. Territorial Scope

140. Israeli law applies to its territory, including East Jerusalem, annexed in 1967, and to the Golan Heights, annexed in 1981, despite broad international disagreement. The EU's adequacy decision regarding Israel excludes these regions from its scope.[182]

---

176. For discussion, *see* T. Morse, *Covering the Dead*, 15(1) Journalism Stud. 98 (2014).
177. LCA 1917/92 *Skoler v. Gerbi*, 57(5) PD 764, 772 (1993).
178. Birnhack, *Private Space*, *supra* n. 174, at 132–135.
179. OM (Tel Aviv, District) 50725-02-12 *Schwartzman v. Psagot Savings and Pension Ltd.* (2012).
180. OM (Tel Aviv, Magistrate) 29490-05-12 *Estate of Doe v. Feldman-Koppler* (2012).
181. For discussion in the Israeli context, *see* M. Birnhack & T. Morse, *Digital Remains: What Happens to Our Personal Data after We Die?* (ISOC 2018), at https://www.isoc.org.il/wp-content/uploads/2019/10/digital-remains-ENG.pdf (Report in Hebrew; Summary in English).
182. Commission Decision of 31 Jan. 2011 pursuant to Directive 95/46/EC of the European Parliament and of the Council on the adequate protection of personal data by the State of Israel with regard to automated processing of personal data.

141. The PPA applies to any person within the territory: citizens and residents, but also asylum seekers, refugees, and tourists. The Basic Law: Human Dignity and Liberty and the PPA use the term 'person' without qualifications. This application reflects the principle of territoriality, namely, that Israeli law applies within Israel.

142. In the few situations in which Israeli law does have an extra-territorial reach, usually based on the citizenship status of the person, it seems that the PPA would apply as well. There has been no case law on the matter. For example, as of 2002, Israeli tax law is based on a personal basis rather than a territorial basis; thus, Israelis should report and pay taxes for income earned and received abroad.[183] The Israeli tax authority should respect the privacy of Israeli citizens also when they are abroad.

143. Foreign and migrant workers need to receive a permit to enter and work in Israel.[184] The law that regulates this field clarifies that it is without prejudice to any other law.[185] The Supreme Court clarified that although foreign workers are not subject to the full range of rights and duties that apply to citizens and residents, they are entitled to the protection of fundamental legal principles as long as they are in Israeli territory.[186] This scope, the Court added, applied also to illegal migrants. In practice, however, foreign employees enjoy less privacy. For example, since 2004 the State operates a national biometric database for foreign workers (as well as asylum seekers and refugees), without any statutory basis, which now contains data of more than 500,000 people. The State committed to enact a law in this regard;[187] the State Comptroller has also called for such legislation[188] – but so far, none has been legislated.

144. The PPA does not refer to the identity or location of the data controller. For those controllers who operate from within Israel, the law applies. For those that operate from a foreign country – the law is silent. The general principle of territoriality applies here, namely, that Israeli law applies in Israel. Conventional principles of private international law (a.k.a. conflict of laws) apply here. Accordingly, the challenge is to determine which jurisdiction has the power to adjudicate a case and under which law.

145. The issue becomes more complicated, as the interaction of Israeli data subjects and foreign service providers is simultaneously subject to several legal fields: privacy (and data protection) law, contract law, and consumer law, and on occasion, additional bodies of law. Under privacy law, and given that the PPA is a tort-based Act, the choice of law should generally follow the concept of *lex loci delicti*, i.e.,

183. Tax Ordinance [New Version], s. 2.
184. According to the Foreign Workers Act, 1991, s. 1M, and The Entrance to Israel Act, 1952, ss 2(c), 3A, 10A.
185. Foreign Workers Act, 1991, s. 1C.
186. HCJ 11437/05 *Workers' Hotline v. Ministry of Interior*, 64(3) PD 111, 160–162 (2011).
187. HCJ 6129/11 *Center for Assistance to Foreign Workers v. Population and Immigration Authority* (2012).
188. 70B State Comptroller Annual Report, 276–282 (2020).

the place where the wrong has occurred. Under contract law, the jurisdiction and the choice of law are to be determined by the parties to the contract and the general affinity of the contract to a specific jurisdiction under the circumstances.

146. However, Israeli contract law also contains the Standard Contracts Act, 1982, which allows courts to interfere with regard to unduly disadvantageous conditions. Applying this statutory power, in *Facebook Inc. v. Ben Hammo*, the Supreme Court found that Facebook Ireland's determination in its terms of use, that Californian courts have sole jurisdiction, was disadvantageous.[189] Yet, the Court found that the contractual stipulation that the applicable law was that of California was not disadvantageous. Subsequent District Court decisions generally followed this precedent and applied the laws of England,[190] Texas,[191] and Hong Kong.[192]

147. In yet other cases, courts interpreted the contract at stake according to Israeli contract law, in order to determine, for instance, whether small Israeli businesses were to be regarded as 'consumers' or businesses, which would determine the applicable law.[193] The Supreme Court then ruled that Facebook's determination that applicable law is that of California was disadvantageous under the Standard Contracts Act, when plaintiff was an individual or a small business.[194] The latter term – 'small business' – is not defined in the law or in the contract; hence the Court remanded the case to the lower court to make a factual determination. The Court distinguished these situations from class actions that are based on privacy claims.[195]

148. Under a tort perspective, searching for the place where the tort took place raises further challenges. Following the lifecycle of information, if the wrong relates to the physical collection of data from data subjects who are in Israel, the tort occurs in Israel, and Israeli law would apply. Processing data, a term that is not fully defined in this context in Israeli law,[196] is the next stage. If 'processing' includes collecting, initial processing and transferring data, these may take place 'in Israel' or 'outside Israel', but this is fact-specific determination and may yield confusing results. Additional processing activities that take place may thus escape Israeli law. These determinations may require deciding where the database is – artificially extending physical notions to the online context. If the database is created in Israel, additional duties may apply, such as the duty to register the database with the Registrar, if the PPA's conditions are met. To date, there is no binding precedent on the matter.

---

189. LCA 5860/16 *Facebook Inc. v. Ben Hammo* (2018).
190. Class A. (Central District) 54491-01-15 *Bashan v. Easyjet PLC* (2020).
191. LCA 4761/04 *Hotels.com v. Zuz Tourism Ltd.* (2005).
192. Class A. (Central District) 9139-05-18 *Tzvia v. Agoda Company Pte. Ltd.* (2022).
193. *See, e.g.*, LCA 8160/20 *Google LL.C. v. Eshel* (2022).
194. LCA 1901/20 *Troim Miller Ltd. v. Facebook Ireland Ltd.* (2022).
195. *Ibid.*, at para. 41 of Justice Groskopf's opinion.
196. For discussion of this point, *see* Part II, Ch. 3.

§5. TERRITORIAL SCOPE: THE WEST BANK

149. Israeli law does not apply per se in the West Bank. The applicable law in that region is complex, and composed of several layers, with some differences regarding Israeli settlers who live in the area and Palestinians who live there. International law imposes various duties on the military commander of the region, according to which extensive security-legislation was put in place. The Israeli Supreme Court has added another legal layer – that of administrative law.[197] According to the Court's long-standing jurisprudence, the Israeli commanders governing in the West Bank are subject to Israeli administrative law, and hence, this body of law is carried over to the West Bank.

150. Israeli settlers are subject to most of Israeli law, either on a personal jurisdiction basis, or through extra-territorial mechanisms that extend Israeli law to apply to them. The Supreme Court has also applied the Basic Laws to review Israeli legislation that affected settlers in the West Bank,[198] as well as commands by the military commander.[199]

151. Palestinians who live in the region are subject to international law, human rights law, Israeli administrative law, and Israeli security-based commands, but are not subject to Israeli constitutional law. The Court has repeatedly avoided the complex question of whether Palestinians should enjoy rights under Israeli Basic Laws,[200] and turns to the previous legal layers.[201] An affirmative decision in this regard may have broad political implications. In practice, Palestinians are subject to numerous covert and overt surveillance schemes.[202]

---

197. *See, e.g.*, HCJ 393/82 *Jam'iat Iscan Al-Ma'almoun v. IDF Commander in the Judea and Samaria Area*, 37(4) PD 785, 809 (1983).

198. HCJ 1661/05 *Regional Council Gaza Region v. Israel Knesset*, 59(2) PD 481, 560 (2005).

199. HCJ 7957/04 *Mara'abe v. The Prime Minister of Israel*, 60(2) PD 477 (2006).

200. *See, e.g.*, Y. Ronen, *The Applicability of Basic Law: Human Dignity and Liberty in the West Bank*, 7 Sha'arey Mishpat 149 (2014) [Hebrew]; A. Shinar, *Israel's External Constitution: Friends, Enemies, and the Constitutional/Administrative Law Distinction*, 57 Va. J. Inte'l L. 735 (2018).

201. *See, e.g.*, HCJ 2189/20 *Hamed v. IDF Commander in the West Bank* (2021). The petition challenged a security-based command, permitting searches of home without a judicial warrant. The Court reviewed the Geneva Convention, 1949 and the security commands, and mentioned Israeli administrative law, without turning to the Israeli Basic Laws.

202. *See* O. Ben-Naftali, *X-Rays*, in *The ABC of the OPT: A Legal Lexicon of the Israeli Control over the Occupied Palestinian Territory* 475, 480–487 (O. Ben-Naftali, M. Sfard & H. Viterbo eds, Cambridge U. Press 2018); H. Viterbo, *Future-Oriented Measures*, in *The ABC of the OPT: A Legal Lexicon of the Israeli Control over the Occupied Palestinian Territory* 118, 135–136 (O. Ben-Naftali, M. Sfard & H. Viterbo eds, Cambridge U. Press 2018).

Chapter 3. Concepts and Definitions

§1. Introduction

152. The PPA provides for key concepts and definitions that affect the material scope of the Act and the judicial interpretation thereof. These are especially important given that the PPA is largely outdated and courts often have to interpret it in light of new technological scenarios not envisaged by the legislature at the time.

153. Some key concepts resonate with well-known privacy and data protection concepts in other jurisdictions and modern legislation such as the GDPR, due the background of the PPA and the cultural and legal culture it is rooted in.[203] However, due to the patchwork structure of the PPA, and the fact that it sometimes conflates traditional privacy torts and data protection concepts, some of these key concepts either overlap or are incoherent. In addition, some key concepts discussed below remain without statutory definition, which at times furthers the incoherence but also leaves room for judicial development and interpretation of the PPA.[204]

§2. General Concepts

Infringement of privacy

154. A key concept under the PPA is infringement of privacy. Section 2 of the PPA sets forth twelve instances that constitute infringement of traditional privacy torts (which are also set as criminal offences):

(1) Spying on or trailing a person in a manner likely to harass him, or any other harassment;
(2) listening-in prohibited under any Law;
(3) Photographing a person while he is in the private domain;
(4) Publishing a person's photograph under such circumstances that the publication is likely to humiliate him or bring him into contempt;
(4A) Publishing a victim's photograph in public, taken at the time of harm or immediately thereafter, in a manner allowing his or her identification and in circumstance that may cause embarrassment, excluding the publication of a photo without delay between the photography and the actual broadcasting that is not unreasonable given the circumstances; for these purposes 'victim' means whomever suffered physical or mental harm due to an unexpected event and whose damage is visible;
(5) Copying or using, without permission from the addressee or writer, the contents of a letter or any other writing not intended for publication,

203. *See* discussion in Part II, Ch. 2.
204. For convenience, when addressing key concepts and definitions below, we will sometimes use terms associated with parallel concepts in well-known data protection legislation, although these do not necessarily correspond with the exact translation or concept under the PPA.

unless the writing is of historical value or fifteen years have passed since the time of writing. In this section 'writing' – including electronic message as defined in Electronic Signature Law, 2001;

(6) Using a person's name, appellation, picture or voice for profit;
(7) Infringing a duty of secrecy laid down by law in respect of a person's private affairs;
(8) Infringing a duty of secrecy laid down by express or implicit agreement in respect of a person's private affairs;
(9) Using, or passing on to another, information on a person's private affairs otherwise than for the purpose for which it was given;
(10) Publishing or delivering anything obtained by way of an infringement of privacy under paragraphs (1) to (7) or (9);
(11) Publishing any matter relating to a person's intimate life, including his sexual history, state of health or conduct in the private domain.

155. As readily apparent from this list, some of its provisions pertain to physical privacy and correspond to the 1981 form of the PPA. Other provisions, such as subsection (6), resemble the right of publicity.[205] However, certain provisions are technologically agnostic and can be relatively easily applied to modern processing of personal data.

156. Note that the different privacy torts refer to different stages in the lifecycle of data: section 2(1), dealing with harassment, refers to the manner of data collection; sections 2(2) (wiretapping), 2(3) (photographing in a private domain) pertain to data collection, sections 2(4) and 2(4A) (publishing photographs), 2(5) (dealings with letters), 2(7) and 2(8) breach of confidentiality duties), 2(10) (publishing privacy infringing material) and 2(11) (publishing intimate data) deal with publication, including transfer to others. Sections 2(5) (dealings with letters), 2(6) (appropriation of personality), and 2(9) (purpose limitation) also deal with using the data already accessed or collected.

157. This observation matters. In a medical negligence case in which an expert witness submitted medical documents of another patient, unrelated to the case, with their name deleted, the court distinguished between the use of the data, namely, submitting it as evidence in an unidentifiable manner, and the way in which it was obtained in the first place.[206] For the publication stage, the Court found that no infringement took place and remanded the case to the lower court to discuss the prior stage of obtaining the data.

205. However, s. 2(6) is not identical to a right to publicity. When McDonald's used a news report that included the name of a well-known basketball player, Ariel McDonald, the Court found that the player has himself commercialized his name (in ads for Burger King); hence s. 2(6) was irrelevant to him. CA 8483/02 *Aloniell Ltd. v. McDonald*, 58(4) PD 314 (2004). The Court reserved the specific privacy tort to situations in which no other interest but privacy was harmed.

206. LCA 7828/17 *Hadassah Medical Organization v. Doe* (2018).

158. In particular, sub-sections (1) and (9) are relevant not only to privacy torts but also to data protection instances as well and we discuss them in greater length.

159. Section 2(1) generally focuses on surveillance. It acknowledges that surveillance, in and of itself, may infringe privacy rights of individuals. Most judicial cases discussing this section have focused on physical surveillance.[207] However, the agnostic language of this sub-section which focuses on 'spying' or 'trailing' of a person can potentially apply to technological circumstances. So far, no substantial cases were decided on this point. It may well be that technological monitoring of individuals constitutes the infringement of privacy under section 2(1). However, given that this sub-section requires another element, i.e., likelihood of harassment, not any act of monitoring constitutes such infringement.[208] Additional laws specifically protect against sexual harassment,[209] stalking,[210] and spam.[211]

160. Section 2(9) is one of the constituent elements of the purpose limitation principle under the PPA.[212] It explicitly sets forth that any use of information regarding the private affairs of a person, other than for the purpose for which it was provided, infringes privacy. The term 'private affairs of a person' (which appears also in sections 2(7), 2(8)) remains undefined. Courts have interpreted and applied it on an ad hoc basis.

Ramifications

161. A finding of prima facie infringement of privacy may lead to Chapter C of the PPA, which contains various defences that the defendant or accused may raise. A finding that evidence was obtained by infringing privacy may lead to the evidence excluded under section 32.

162. Infringement of privacy under section 2 is a tort (section 4), and if done maliciously, regarding sections 2(1), 2(3)–2(7), 2(9)–2(11), it constitutes a criminal offence (section 5). The two privacy violations which do not comprise a criminal offence under the PPA are wiretapping under section 2(2), which is separately addressed in the Wiretapping Act, and section 2(8), which addressed breach of a contractual duty of confidentiality.[213]

---

207. *See, e.g.*, CA 145/80 *Vaknin v. Beit Shemesh Municipality*, 37(1) PD 113 (1982); LCA 2558/16 *Jane Doe v. Compensation Officer – Ministry of Defence* (2017); Crim. A. 4743/20 *Leybel v. State of Israel* (2022).

208. For a Magistrate court decision determining that publishing a family photo publicly included in a person's social media account may be deemed as harassing monitoring, *see* CC (Kfar Saba, Magistrate) 22616-02-21 *Kleimann v. Kelsch*, para. 45 (2022).

209. Prevention of Sexual Harassment Act, 1998.

210. Prevention of Intimidating Harassment Act, 2002.

211. *See* s. 30A of the Communications Act (Telecommunications and Broadcasting), 1982, and discussion in Part I, Ch. 3 above.

212. *See also* Part III, Ch. 1 below.

213. *See also* Part VIII, Chs 4–6, which discuss these issues in greater detail.

Personal Data

163. As explained above, the basic unit of the data protection chapter of the PPA is a 'database'. The definition of a database, as further discussed below, is based on the definition of 'data' (or 'information'). The term 'personal data' does not appear in the PPA. In fact, it is a concept that is compounded by two separate terms, appearing in two separate parts of the PPA. In Chapter A of the PPA, the constituent term, appearing in section 2(9) dealing with purpose limitation violations, is 'information on the private affairs of a person,' which we discuss below. In Chapter B of the PPA, the constituent term, defined in section 7 of the PPA and applicable to the data protection part of it, is 'data', defined as 'data on the personality, personal status, intimate affairs, state of health, economic position, vocational qualifications, opinions and beliefs of a person'. While these two terms – 'private affairs' and 'data' – are placed in separate chapters of the PPA and technically do not have a statutory link, courts and the PP Authority often conflate them,[214] and the interpretation of the former is at times used to interpret the latter, and vice versa.

164. Accordingly, the concept of 'data' is a key feature of the PPA. It triggers the applicability of key provisions of the PPA, both the privacy tort and the data protection ones. The purpose limitation infringement of section 2(9) is only triggered when information of a private affairs of a person is at stake. The provisions pertaining to processing of personal data are triggered only when data, as defined in section 7 of the PPA, is concerned. However, due to the fact that the PPA does not define the first term, and the second term is defined in a manner inconsistent with modern understanding of data protection, some uncertainty remains regarding the scope of the concept of personal data, especially in more complex technological circumstances.

165. Whereas core types of personal data such as financial status, medical status, sexual orientation or conduct, and political and religious beliefs are either explicitly listed as 'data' for data protection purposes, or have been interpreted to be information on private affairs of a person, other types of personal data have not yet been fully or explicitly addressed by courts. This is mainly due to the fact that these terms bear a strong content-based criterion, and a more subtle identification-based criterion.[215] In specific circumstances, the Supreme Court explained that information on private affairs of a person could be established where reverse engineering of data could reveal the identity of the individual, namely, when the subject can be re-identified.[216] Courts, however, have not yet decided whether online unique identifiers pass the threshold of 'data'. For example, in the context of location data,

214. *See, e.g.*, Privacy Protection Authority, Legal Opinion, *What are 'Data' and 'Information on a Person's Private Affairs' According to the Privacy Protection Law* (May 2021).
215. *See* discussion in Part II, Ch. 2 above.
216. CA 1697/11 *Gottesman Architecture Ltd. v. Vardi* (2013).

several courts, including the Supreme Court, acknowledged that location data constitutes 'private affairs of a person' in certain circumstances.[217] And while this extension to the concept of 'private affairs of a person' is applied to Chapter A of the PPA dealing with privacy torts, reading it under the term 'data' is yet to be decided.[218]

Processing of Personal Data

166. A 'database' is defined as digital collection of data (as defined in the PPA). This means that the entire concept of processing of personal data generally applies only to *digital* processing of data. Except for this explicit limitation, the PPA does not include a robust definition for the term 'processing'; the Act does include certain references to the 'use' of personal data which is a more limited term, compared to modern data protection legislations.

167. When use of data included in databases is concerned, the PPA provides for a set of rules ranging from database registration duties, data subject rights (being informed, access and rectification), confidentiality and data security duties, cross-border transfer restrictions, and controller-processor relationships.

Controller–Processor Relationship

168. The data protection parts of the PPA clearly recognize the relationship between controllers and processors. While the term data controller is not defined (in fact, the PPA uses the term 'database owner'), the term processor (or 'Data Holder') is, as discussed below. The PPA, the Privacy Protection Regulations (Data Security), 2017 (DataSec Regulations) and guidelines issued by the PP Authority acknowledge the relationship between controllers and processors, apply different duties to each role and mandate certain interactions between them.[219]

Data Subject Rights

169. Where data included in databases is processed, the data subjects are entitled to a set of rights, and controllers (and at times, processors) of such data are under correlative duties. The PPA provides for a right to be informed, a right of access, a right to rectification, and a limited right of erasure, and does not acknowledge the right to object to processing or restrict processing.[220]

Security of Processing

170. The PPA acknowledges the concept of security of processing for the use of data included in databases. The term 'Data Security' is defined as the 'protection of

---

217. *See* AC (Tel Aviv, Admin. Court) 28857-06-17 *Nursing Companies Association v. Ministry of Defence* (2019); HCJ 6732/20 *Association for Civil Rights in Israel v. The Knesset* (2021).

218. *See* Privacy Protection Authority, Legal Opinion, *Does a Collection of Names and Email Addresses Constitute a 'Database'?* (November 2018).

219. *See* Part V.

220. *See* Part IV.

the integrity of the data, or protection of the data from being exposed, used or copied, without lawful permission' (section 7). This definition, and the concept itself, does not cover data availability, which affects some of the duties imposed on controllers and processors.

171. Section 17 of the PPA determines that controllers and processors are each liable for the data security of data included in a database. Regulations promulgated under the PPA, set forth a list of technical and organizational duties imposed on controllers and processors with respect to their Databases.[221]

Anonymous Data

172. The PPA does not explicitly acknowledge the concept of anonymization of personal data. Given that both the terms 'data' and 'information about a person's private affairs' are comprised of an identification-based criterion, it seems clear that data originally collected in a non-identifiable manner does not fall under the PPA. However, the status of de-identified or anonymized data remains unclear and courts have yet to address whether identifiable data, once anonymized, are subject to the PPA and its various requirements.

§3. Key Definitions

173. This Section reviews key definitions in the PPA and discusses their judicial interpretation, and points out certain key terms that have not been defined.

174. 'Consent'. Consent is defined in the PPA as 'informed, express or implied consent' (section 3). This is a limited formulation compared to its European counterpart, which, in part, is dictated by the fact that consent is the only legal basis for processing under the PPA.[222] When judicially reviewed, the key element of consent that has been challenged is whether such consent was informed. Courts opined differently on what the consent language and mechanism should include to constitute 'informed' consent, and have not yet fully addressed this.[223]

175. 'Use'. The privacy torts Chapter of the PPA defines 'use' in a non-conclusive manner: 'Use – includes disclosure, transfer and delivery' (section 3). Courts have not yet weighed in on the scope of interpretation of the term in either privacy torts or in the context of data protection. While in many cases, there will not be any controversy as to what the term means, especially when direct processing, disclosure, or transfer of data are concerned, it leaves open other actions pertaining to data, such as viewing. For example, in declining to approve a class action

221. *See* Part V, Ch. 4 below.
222. *See* discussion in Part III, Ch. 2 below.
223. CA 439/88 *Databases Register v. Ventura*, 48(3) PD 808, 822–826 (1994); LA (National) 90/08 *Issakov-Inbar v. State of Israel – The Commissioner for the Women's Labour Law* (2011), para. 28; CA (Jerusalem, District) 56065-03-21 *Yeffe Nof Transportation Infrastructure and Construction Ltd. v. State of Israel – Ministry of Transportation and Road Safety* (2022).

against Facebook, following a data breach, a court explained that the term 'use' is confined to direct voluntary actions of the controller or processor, rather than to unauthorized third party's access to the data. The hacker's actions did not constitute 'use' by the controller or processor.[224] However, the non-exhaustive nature of the definition allows courts to interpret it broadly. The scope of the term affects various provisions of the PPA, including the purpose limitation provisions (sections 2(9) and 8(b)), and the definition of Processor.

176. 'Processor'. The term is defined in the PPA as 'a person who has a database in his possession permanently and is permitted to use it'. This is a narrow conception of a data processor as it is limited to entities having possession over databases permanently. The definition opens a debate regarding third parties that have remote access to databases and thus arguably do not have possession over it, or third parties that have access or possession of either partial or full segments of databases for a limited duration of time. Courts have not yet addressed these issues and they remain open. We note that section 15 of the DataSec Regulations includes certain provisions addressing the relationship between controllers and third parties who have any type of access to their Databases, and thus partially extend the concept of data processor to additional circumstances more compatible with modern data protection principles, but this is largely limited to data security-related concerns.

177. 'Controller'. While the term 'controller' (or 'owner of a database') is used throughout the data protection provisions of the PPA, there is no definition of the term. It is commonly accepted that controller should have the meaning attributed to the term in well-known data protection legislation, such as the GDPR, i.e., the entity controlling the processing of personal data. A recent bill to amend the PPA, proposed to define the term controller along these lines. However, the bill has not yet been enacted.[225]

178. 'Private Affairs of a Person'. Private affairs of a person is a key term in Chapter A of the PPA, dealing with privacy torts. Especially, it is a key for determining the purpose limitation principle under section 2(9). Nevertheless, the PPA does not define it. Thus, courts have interpreted the meaning of this term on an ad-hoc basis. The Supreme Court's first encounter with the term led to two views. Justice Gabriel Bach offered a broad interpretation: 'The natural and ordinary meaning of the words 'private affairs' of a person means any information pertaining to the private life of that person, including his name, address, phone number, workplace, the identity of his friends, his relationship with his wife and other family members, and the like.'[226] Justice Tova Strassberg-Cohen was more cautious at the

---

224. *See* Class. A. (Tel Aviv, District) 7322-10-18 *Axelrod v. Facebook Inc.* (2022).
225. Bill for Protection of Privacy (Amendment No. 14), 2022.
226. CA 439/88 *Databases Register v. Ventura*, 48(3) PD 808, 821 (1994).

time, but opted for a context-based interpretation.[227] Interestingly, she mentioned that while separate pieces of data may not harm privacy, their combination may, thus anticipating digital practices.[228]

179. In the above case, the data subject was identified. In subsequent cases, the Court has extended the term to cover also infringements pertaining to data that were not directly identifying an individual but could, after reverse engineering, identify them.[229] These decisions dealt with offline situations. Therefore, it remains to be seen whether any potentially identifiable information constitutes 'private affairs of a person' or only those identifiable data that are also in the core of a person's privacy.[230]

180. 'Data'. Data is defined in the PPA as 'data on the personality, personal status, intimate affairs, state of health, economic position, vocational qualifications, opinions and beliefs of a person'. This definition only applies to Chapter B of the PPA, which deals with data protection, and not to Chapter A, which focuses on privacy torts. Since this definition is also content-based, it may leave out certain types of personal data and exclude them from data protection. The PP Authority has issued an opinion as to the interpretation of this term, which opts for a broad scope, covering also identifiable data as opposed to covering only directly identifying data.[231] Courts have seldom addressed this definition. When defendant, a restaurant reservation service, exposed email addresses to other subscribers, a magistrate court found that given the subscribers' consent to the service's terms and conditions, that permitted transfer of data to third parties, email addresses were not considered private affairs of a person.[232]

181. 'Database'. A database means 'a collection of data, kept by a magnetic or optic means and intended for computer processing, except – (1) a collection for personal use that is not for business purposes; or (2) a collection that includes only the name, address and method of communication, which in itself does not produce a characterization which infringes the privacy of the persons whose names are included therein, provided that the owner of the collection or the body corporate under his control does not have another collection' (section 7). This means that databases for personal use and manual, non-digital collections of data are excluded from

227. *Ibid.*, at 835.
228. *Ibid.*
229. CA 1697/11 *Gottesman Architecture Ltd. v. Vardi* (2013).
230. *See* HCJ 3809/08 *Association for Civil Rights in Israel v. Israel Police* (2012), para. 7; Class. A. (Central District, District) 22141-03-15 *Greenberg v. Cellcom Israel Ltd.* (2020). *See also* Privacy Protection Authority, Legal Opinion, *What Are 'Data' and 'Information on a Person's Private Affairs' According to the Privacy Protection Law* (May 2021).
231. Privacy Protection Authority, Legal Opinion, *What Are 'Data' and 'Information on a Person's Private Affairs' According to the Privacy Protection Law* (May 2021).
232. Class. A. (Tel Aviv, Magistrate) 39798-11-15 *Galanti v. Y.N.M. Round Tables Concepts Ltd.* (2016).

the definition. Another exclusion is for databases that only include names and contact information, but only in cases where the controller does not have other databases that could be correlated with and enrich such collections.[233] This means that only controllers of purely communicative collections of data, without any further data regarding the data subjects (including their purchase histories), may enjoy this exemption.

182. 'Data Security'. Data Security is defined in the PPA as 'protection of the integrity of the data, or protection of the data from being exposed, used or copied, without lawful permission'. The definition affects both potential civil liability for data breaches as well as the scope of the regulatory security requirements under the DataSec Regulations.

233. *See also* LCA 3351/16 *Vasserman v. Klein* (2016) para. 7; CA (Tel Aviv, District) 22526/06 *Israel Bar Association v. Ayalon Insurance Company Ltd.*, 4–6 (2006); Privacy Protection Authority, Legal Opinion, *What are 'Data' and 'Information on a Person's Private Affairs' According to the Privacy Protection Law* (May 2021).

Part III. General Principles

Chapter 1. Data Quality Principles

§1. Introduction

183. Unlike Article 5 of the GDPR, the PPA does not include declaratory provisions pertaining to data quality or processing principles. However, its various provisions, alongside respective regulations and guidelines issued by the PP Authority, and judicial interpretation, do provide for certain *substantive* data quality principles. We discuss these in this chapter vis-à-vis well-known data quality principles in modern data protection laws.

§2. Purpose Limitation

184. The PPA addresses the purpose limitation principle both regarding privacy torts (PPA, Chapter A) and its data protection regime (PPA, Chapter B). While the underlying principle is similar, the actual provisions vary between the two contexts, in scope and substance.

185. The purpose limitation principle in the privacy tort context appears in section 2(9). It explicitly sets forth that any use of data regarding the private affairs of a person, other than for the purpose for which they were provided, infringes privacy. However, the term 'private affairs of a person' remains undefined, and thus courts ruled on an ad-hoc basis with interpreting it, although they do tend to interpret it broadly.[234]

186. For example, in a leading case, an insurance company challenged the PP Authority's decision that using data on a person's civil foreclosure registered with the insurance company for underwriting purposes, infringes the purpose limitation principle of sections 2(9) and 8(b) of the PPA. The insurance company argued that data on such foreclosure lawfully received under the Bankruptcy Act, 1967, should not be considered 'private affairs' or 'Data,' and that it has a legitimate interest in using such data for underwriting purposes. The Administrative court declined the petition, explaining the importance of the right to privacy and the centrality of the purpose limitation principle. The court ruled that data on civil foreclosure was

234. *See* discussion in Part II, Ch. 3 above.

indeed a person's private affairs. The court further ruled that the purpose for which the data were provided to the insurance company under the Bankruptcy Act was to secure the collection of debts rather than for underwriting considerations.[235]

187. Section 2(9) does not explicitly address circumstances where personal data were obtained by the controller from a third party who is not the data subject. However, when personal data were obtained by a third party and were used for purposes that were incompatible with the original purposes, courts decided that the purpose limitation principle under section 2(9) applied.[236] This is especially relevant to publicly available data at the choice of the data subject, which may have been published for certain purposes but later collected by third parties for their own separate purposes. Conceivably, and without alternative legal bases for processing other than consent,[237] such conduct constitutes infringement of privacy.

188. A major flaw in current Israeli law in this regard, is that the PPA does not limit the purpose for which data may be obtained, other than illegal purposes. Public bodies as well as employers are limited in this regard and the purposes should be 'legitimate'. However, a private entity may collect data for any legal purpose, and may phrase it in broad terms. A proposal to limit the purposes to legitimate purposes only was rejected by the Schoffman Committee.[238]

189. Accordingly, while the purpose limitation principle embedded in section 2(9) focuses on the purposes for which personal data were provided, the general concept of consent may override the principle: If consent (as defined in the PPA) was obtained to repurpose the personal data, such conduct would be allowed and would not infringe privacy.

190. As for the data protection part of the PPA, the purpose limitation principle appears in section 8(b), which states that 'a person shall not use information in a database that requires registration under this section except for the purpose for which the database was established'. This provision includes certain qualifications.

191. First, this provision only applies to the use of data included in databases (defined in the PPA, section 7), and therefore does not apply to manual non-digital processing of personal data or to circumstances excluded from such definitions (which then may come under section 2(9)).

192. Second, the provision only applies to databases that require registration.[239]

235. AC (Tel Aviv, District) 24867-02-11 *IDI Insurance Co. Ltd. v. Database Registrar* (2012).
236. CA 439/88 *Databases Register v. Ventura*, 48(3) PD 808 (1994).
237. *See* discussion in Part III, Ch. 2 below.
238. Committee for Reviewing Legislation in the Area of Databases (J. Schoffman, Chair, Jerusalem 2007). One of the current authors (Birnhack) who was a member of the committee, remained in dissent in that regard.
239. *See* discussion in Part V, Ch. 1 on database registration obligations and exclusions thereof.

193. Third, and most importantly, the key element of the purpose limitation provision in section 8(b) is the purpose that the database owner stated when registering the database (section 9(b)(2)), and not necessarily the purpose conveyed to the data subject, to which they consented. Recall that under section 2(9), the purpose limitation principle is assessed according to the subject's consent, which should be informed, i.e., it is based on the information conveyed to the subject prior to collecting the personal data. This duty complemented by the duty to notify data subjects of the purpose of processing under section 11, the violation of which is an independent tort. Note that a data controller should meet both versions of the purpose limitation principle as well as the duty to notify the data subject. Hence, in practice, even if there is a gap between the registered purposes (which tends to use broad language) and the ones conveyed to data subjects (which tend to be somewhat more specific), the data controller should not deviate from either the registered purpose or the specific purpose conveyed to the subject, nor may it process data in contrast to the purposes set forth in the data subject notification.

§3. Proportionality

194. The PPA does not include a proportionality principle. As discussed below, the only legal basis for processing personal data under the PPA is consent, and in some specific instances explicit legal authority, without considering proportionality.

195. However, in certain specific circumstances, Israeli law does provide for proportionality principles in the context of processing of personal data, especially where inherent imbalance of powers between controllers and data subjects exists. One such context is the vertical one, when the data controller is a public body or another kind of body which is subject to constitutional privacy rules.[240]

196. Another context in which proportionality applies, is employment relationship.[241] Israeli Labour Courts often deem consent to be suspicious and thus seek additional indications of adequate dealing between employers and employees (including candidates).[242] In the specific context of processing of personal data, the National Labour Court has consistently ruled that employees' consent to data processing is always suspicious and thus, to demonstrate lawful processing of personal data, employers should prove that their processing is also proportionate to the intended purposes.[243]

197. The principle of proportionality is also reflected, to a certain extent, in the general exemption provided to law enforcement agencies under section 19(b) of the

---

240. *See* Part I, Ch. 1.
241. *See* Part IX, Ch. 4.
242. LA (National) 82/07 *Ras Aida v.* Qalansawe *Municipality* (2008) paras 75, 117; LC (National) 4-70/97 *Tel Aviv University v. Histadrut Labour Federation* (1998) para. 22.
243. LA (National) 90/08 *Issakov-Inbar v. The State of Israel – The Commissioner for the Women's Labour Law* (2011); LA (National) 7541-04-14 *New Histadrut (General Organization of Workers in Israel) v. Qalansawe Municipality* (2017).

PPA.[244] The exemption is provided to law enforcement agencies infringing privacy only if such infringement is 'reasonably committed within the scope of their functions and for the purpose of carrying them out'. The concept of reasonableness and fit of purpose in this regard echoes the proportionality principle.

198. In consumer-related cases, there may be a link between the concept of consent under the PPA and the general law pertaining to standard form contracts. The Israeli Standard Contract Act, 1982, provides that certain conditions in non-negotiable (namely, in the form of 'take it or leave it') standard contracts between businesses and customers are either void or could be voided by courts if determined to be depriving towards customers (section 3). While this Act does not refer to privacy or data protection, privacy policies and statements may be considered a standard contract, and hence subject to the principles of the specific Act. This means that courts may invalidate unfair provisions. Indeed, in the context of Facebook's terms of use, the Supreme Court ruled that the stipulation on choice of jurisdiction (listing California as the exclusive jurisdiction) was void.[245] The key question under standard contract doctrine would be whether such provisions grant unfair advantage to the business. When courts review petitions to void depriving conditions, they apply a balancing test that considers the balance or imbalance of power between the parties, the allegedly unfair or depriving condition, and the legitimate business purpose. This is mainly a question of proportionality.[246]

§4. Fairness and Transparency

199. Fairness, as a general principle, is not included in the PPA at all, nor was it considered by courts as a principle for the lawfulness of processing of personal data. However, acting in good faith is an overarching principle in Israeli law as mandated by sections 39 and 61(b) of the Contracts Act (General Part), 1973.[247] This may inform the contents of 'fairness', and provide the legal anchor. At present, there has been no case law on the matter.

200. Transparency, is explicitly acknowledged in the PPA, both in its privacy tort Chapter and its data protection Chapter.

201. First, as discussed above, the definition of Consent under the PPA requires such consent to be informed. Courts have interpreted this term differently in various circumstances, but in general, it requires that the manifestation of consent by the

244. *See* discussion in Part X, Ch. 3 below.

245. LCA 5860/16 *Facebook Inc. v. Ben Hammo* (2018).

246. LCA 1901/20 *Troim Miler Ltd. v. Facebook Ireland Ltd.* (2022).

247. *See, e.g.*, LCA 6339/97 *Roker v. Solomon*, 55(1) PD 199, 276–282 (1999); HCJ 164/97 *Kontram Ltd. v. Ministry of Finance*, 52(1) PD 289 (1998).

data subject is based on sufficient information to understand the nature of data processing at stake.[248] If insufficient information is provided to the data subject, consent would be invalid and no legal basis would exist for the processing of personal data.

202. Second, from a data protection perspective, the PPA contains a specific data subject notification duty (section 11), requiring the data controller, when approaching a data subject to collect personal data, to inform the data subject of the purpose of processing, to whom the personal data will be transferred and whether there is legal obligation to provide the personal data.[249] While violating the duty to inform does not necessarily affect the validity of consent for the privacy tort aspects of the PPA, which, as explained above, could also be implicit, such conduct constitutes an independent violation of the data protection provisions of the PPA (section 31B).

§5. Data Minimization and Retention

203. The PPA does not include provisions pertaining specifically to data minimization and retention. However, some legal principles and some specific provisions provide for a limited de facto acknowledgement of the principle.

204. First, a public body and private bodies which are subject to constitutional principles, should act in a proportional manner. Proportionality includes, *inter alia*, the least harmful means norm. Collecting excessive data, beyond what is necessary to achieve the legitimate goal, may be deemed not proportional.[250]

205. Second, the limited data erasure right provides for some limitation on the retention of personal data.[251]

206. Third, the purpose limitation principle in section 2(9) of the tort part of the PPA deems it unlawful to process personal data for purposes other than those for which the data were provided. If such purposes of processing cease to exist, arguably, any additional processing exceeds such purposes and constitutes infringement of privacy.

207. Fourth, section 2(c) of the DataSec Regulations requires any data controller to review and consider, on an annual basis, whether the personal data retained by it is no longer necessary for the purposes for which the database was established. While this section does not explain under which circumstances personal data is no longer necessary for a controller, it implicitly requires controllers to consider

248. HCJ 6732/20 *Association for Civil Rights in Israel v. The Knesset* (2021); CA 439/88 *Databases Register v. Ventura*, 48(3) PD 808, 822–826 (1994).
249. *See* discussion in Part IV, Ch. 1 below. *See also* Privacy Protection Authority, *Obligation to Notify as Part of Collection and Use of Personal Data* (May 2022).
250. *See* Part I, Ch. 1.
251. *See* discussion in Part IV, Ch. 4 below.

their data retention practices and provides some leeway to the PP Authority with respect to the enforcement of this principle.

208. However, a private entity may state their purpose broadly, thus rendering the above less relevant. No case law has examined this possibility.

§6. Data Accuracy

209. The concept of data accuracy is partially acknowledged in the PPA through the relatively weak right of rectification, and the correlative duty to follow the request of the data subject in certain circumstances. Section 14 of the PPA provides data subject with the right to request rectification of their data included in the database (as defined in the PPA), if such data is inaccurate, incomplete, unclear, or outdated. As explained below, the right of rectification is limited and does not form a strong concept of data accuracy.[252]

210. Specific regulations require procedures for assuring data quality in specific contexts. For example, section 17 of the Patients' Rights Act, 1996, requires medical institutions to accurately manage medical records. Another example is found in the guidelines of the Capital Markets, Insurance and Savings Authority, which require various financial institutions to accurately and uniformly present certain financial data to customers.[253]

§7. Data Security

211. The data security principle is well-founded in the PPA, which defines 'Data Security' as 'protection of the integrity of the information, or protection of the information from being exposed, used or copied, without lawful permission' (section 7). This is an old formulation of the concept of data security, which does not explicitly include, for example, data availability that is part of the well-known confidentiality-integrity-availability triad. Both controllers and processors are subject to data security obligations and potential liability under the PPA, and the DataSec Regulations set forth extensive technical and organizational duties that apply to controllers and processors of personal data.[254] We note that the concept of data security under the PPA applies only to the data protection parts of the Act, and as such, applies only to Databases, i.e., digital processing of personal data. However, breach of data security in other contexts, such as manual databases, may be addressed under Chapter A of the PPA, according to the particular circumstances.[255]

---

252. *See* Part IV, Ch. 3 below.
253. Institutional Bodies Guidelines 7-9-2021, Uniform Structure to Transfer Information and Data in the Pension Savings Market.
254. *See* Part V, Ch. 4 below.
255. *See* ss 2(7), 2(8).

Chapter 2. Legal Grounds for Processing Personal Data

§1. Introduction

212. The PPA does not follow the framework of modern data protection legislation and therefore does not explicitly acknowledge a variety of legal grounds for processing of personal data. In fact, the data protection part of the PPA does not address the question of legality of collection or processing of personal data, other than a purpose limitation requirement. On a more substantive level, the PPA provides for two main lawful grounds for the processing of personal data. The primary is consent, and the secondary is through explicit legal authority or duty.

§2. Consent

213. The privacy tort part of the PPA provides for a list of circumstances constituting infringement of privacy, which is prohibited. However, consent, defined in the PPA as informed consent which could be express or implicit, overrides any infringement of privacy and legalizes such conduct.[256]

214. Therefore, consent is the primary and almost exclusive lawful ground for processing of personal data, especially in commercial and civil contexts. It is thus not surprising that the consent requirement under the PPA is relatively lax in comparison to modern data protection legislation that offer additional lawful grounds for processing such as the performance of contract with the data subject or the legitimate interest of the controller.

215. The fact that consent could be obtained either explicitly or implicitly renders the processing of personal data under the PPA, and the clearing of infringements of privacy, relatively easy for the data controllers. When judicially reviewed, the key element of consent that is being challenged is whether such consent was informed. Courts opined differently on what the consent language and mechanism should include to constitute 'informed' consent.[257] While courts acknowledged that online terms and conditions could be binding in 'click-wrap' and 'registration-wrap' setting in consumer-related circumstances, as explained below, courts have not yet opined on whether information on data processing could be included in more general documents such as privacy policies and terms and conditions.

256. *See* discussion in Part II, Ch. 3 above.

257. CA 439/88 *Databases Register v. Ventura*, 48(3) PD 808, 822–826 (1994); LA (National) 90/08 *Issakov-Inbar v. State of Israel – The Commissioner for the Women's Labour Law* (2011), para. 28; CA (Jerusalem, District) 56065-03-21 *Yeffe Nof Transportation Infrastructure and Construction Ltd. v. State of Israel – Ministry of Transportation and Road Safety* (2022).

216. In digital contexts, Israeli courts have generally acknowledged that consent could be obtained by various ways of affirmative manifestation, including 'click-through' and 'sign-in' mechanisms,[258] whereas 'browse-through' mechanisms were, in certain cases, deemed insufficient to substantiate consent.[259] Thus, consent for privacy and data protection purposes does not require an explicit opt-in mechanism, and could be obtained as part of online registration or checkout processes.

217. In certain contexts of imbalance of powers, especially in labour disputes, courts have sought additional requirements that are required in order to allow personal data processing due to the fact that consent was inherently suspicious.[260] In addition, the PP Authority has clarified that for a profiling-based third-party direct mailing service, explicit opt-in consent is required.[261] Consumer protection law in Israel does not require a heightened standard of consent, and courts have acknowledged online forms of express consent in consumer-related cases.[262]

218. In business-consumer relationships, the Standard Contract Act, 1982, also applies. It allows consumers to claim that certain provisions in the standard contract are depriving, in a manner that provides the business with unfair advantage, and hence are voidable.[263] While this doctrine cannot function as a way to render void the general consent of a consumer to the entire legal document (e.g., terms and conditions or privacy policy), it may render certain excessive provisions in such documents void, and thus the respective excessive data processing may be infringing. The test that courts should consider in such cases is whether the business has a legitimate business interest in including such provisions in the contract, vis-à-vis the types of services provided to the consumer, and what would be considered as adequate in Israeli society.[264]

219. The 'informed' consent requirement is coupled with the data protection notification duty included in section 11 of the PPA, which requires that certain information be communicated to the data subjects before collecting and processing their personal data. Courts have not yet decided in such cases.

§3. Legal Authority or Duty

220. While the PPA does not explicitly acknowledge legal authority or duty as a legal ground for processing, such a principle is embedded in two separate provisions in the exemptions and defences parts of the Act.

258. Class. A. (Central District) 18763-04-15 *Viva Media Ltd. v. Facebook Ireland Ltd.* (2019); Class. A. (Tel Aviv, District) 27205-05-18 *United Parcel Service. Inc. v. Keinan* (2019).
259. *Viva Media, ibid.*; *United Parcel Service, ibid.*
260. *Issakov-Inbar*; LA (National) 7541-04-14 *New Histadrut (General Organization of Workers in Israel) v. Qalansawe Municipality* (2017).
261. Database Registrar Guideline 2/2017, *Interpretation and Application of the Provisions of the Privacy Protection Law Regarding Direct Mail and Direct Mail Services* (2017).
262. *See, e.g., Viva Media*; *United Parcel Service.*
263. Standard Form Contracts Act, 1982, s. 3.
264. LCA 5860/16 *Facebook Inc. v. Ben Hammo* (2018), para. 23; LCA 1901/20 *Troim Miller Ltd. v. Facebook Ireland Ltd.* (2022), paras 23–24, 48.

221. Section 18(2)(b) of the PPA provides that 'in any criminal or civil proceeding for infringement of privacy, it shall be a good defence if one of the following is the case: . . . (2) the defendant or accused committed the infringement in good faith and in any of the following circumstances: . . . (b) the infringement was committed in circumstances in which the infringer was under a legal, moral, social or professional obligation to commit it'.

222. This effectively means that controllers and processors of personal data, acting in good faith and under a legal obligation, do not infringe privacy even if they did not obtain consent which is the primary lawful ground for processing.[265] This is relevant for businesses processing personal data to comply with legal requirements such as meeting employment-related duties, anti-money laundering provisions, tax and accounting duties, etc.

223. In addition, section 19(a) of the PPA provides that 'no person shall bear responsibility under this Law for an act which he is empowered to do by law'. This section mainly applies to governmental entities acting under direct authorization by law, such as law enforcement agencies, and provides a de facto legal ground for processing of personal data for statutory purposes such as publicly available registrars, administrative purposes, etc.

224. Courts have clarified that from an administrative law perspective, section 19 does not create an independent legal authority to process personal data; rather, it applies only if another law provides for such explicit authority.[266]

---

265. Crim. A. 5026/97 *Gal'am v. State of Israel* (1999).
266. HCJ 4455/19 *Tebeka Association v. Israel Police* (2021); CC (Tel Aviv, Magistrate) 50156-06-17 *Musa v. El Al Israel Airways Ltd.* (2022).

Chapter 3. Special Categories of Personal Data

225. The PPA's central unit of reference is that of database, which contains the term 'information' [data] (section 7). The PPA defines 'information' and 'sensitive information' in the following manner.

226. 'Information' means data on the personality, personal status, intimate affairs, state of health, economic position, vocational qualifications, opinions, and beliefs of a person;

227. 'Sensitive Information' means:

(1) data on the personality, intimate affairs, state of health, economic position, opinions, and beliefs of a person;
(2) information that the Minister of Justice determined by Order, with the approval of the Constitution, Law and Justice Committee of the Knesset, is sensitive information.

228. As of writing, no Order was issued under the second clause. The differences between information and sensitive information are minor. The only direct legal implication of the difference is that a database containing sensitive data is subject to the registration duty, regardless of the number of data subjects in the database (section 8(c)(2)).

229. Compared to the GDPR (Article 9), racial and ethnic origin, and trade union membership are not mentioned in the PPA's definitions. However, courts are likely to treat at least the racial and ethnic data as 'information' covered by these definitions, and union membership may be subsumed under 'economic position' as well as 'opinions'.

230. The Supreme Court, in interpreting Chapter A of the PPA, which lists privacy torts, clarified that the legislative list was not exhaustive, and that there may be additional privacy coverage via Common Law.[267] A court treated location data in this manner, as covered by the law.[268]

231. Genetic or biometric data are also not mentioned explicitly but are regulated in specific laws, as discussed above.[269] The National Labour Court treated biometric data (finger scans in that case) as data covered by the law.[270]

267. HCJ 6650/04 *Doe v. Regional Rabbinical Court, Netanya*, 61(1) PD 581 (2006).
268. AC (Tel Aviv, Admin. Court) 28857-06-17 *Caregiving Companies Association v. Ministry of Defence* (2019). An appeal overturned some of the findings, but not those relating to privacy.
269. *See* Part I, Ch. 4.
270. LDA 7541-04-14 *New Histadrut (General Organization of Workers in Israel) v. Qalansawe Municipality* (2017).

Part IV. Data Subject Rights

Chapter 1. Right to Be Informed

§1. SCOPE

232. Section 11 of the PPA imposes a duty to inform a person about the collection, processing and retaining data, to be included in a database. The notice should refer to several elements:

> A request to a person for information with a view to the keeping and use thereof in a database shall be accompanied by a notice indicating –
>
> (1) Whether that person is under a legal duty to deliver that information or whether its delivery depends on his volition and consent;
> (2) The purpose for which the information is requested;
> (3) To whom the information is to be delivered and the purposes of such delivery.

233. The duty imposed on the collecting party creates the data subject's correlative right. The duty and the correlative right are triggered when there is 'data' [information] collected. This term is defined in section 7 to include 'data on the personality, personal status, intimate affairs, state of health, economic position, vocational qualifications, opinions and beliefs of a person'. The duty arises when the data is to be kept in a database, which refers to electronic collections of data (thus excluding manual databases), and excludes databases for personal use or those that contain only name and address.[271]

234. Failing to inform the data subject of the information listed in section 11, or providing inaccurate information is a criminal offence (section 31A(a)(3)),[272] and a civil tort (section 31B).

---

271. For these definitions, *see* Part II, Ch. 3.
272. *See, e.g.*, Crim. C. (Tel Aviv, Magistrate) 006955/98 *State of Israel v. Shacham* (2001) (accused convicted of violating s. 11, for collecting personal data from patients in hospitals, without providing sufficient information, and transferring the medical data to others).

§2. CONSENT

235. Note that the duty to inform, and hence the right to be informed contains an indirect reference to consent, in section 11(1). However, a court specializing in standard contracts explained that consent is not required, since if a person is not interested in providing the data, they may not provide it.[273]

236. Consent is currently the main legal basis for data collection and processing in Israeli law. Section 1 instructs that 'No person shall infringe the privacy of another without his consent.' The upshot is that consent may turn an otherwise privacy violation into a legitimate action. Section 3 defines consent to mean 'informed, express or implied consent', thus tying consent back to the duty to inform.

237. Courts have adopted the interpretation suggested in the literature that informed consent means the data subject's informed decision, based on sufficient information, delivered in a comprehensible manner and made free of any external pressures, especially under conditions of power imbalance.[274]

238. Some courts, especially in the context of labour law, added that consent should be freely given.[275] When there is an inherent imbalance of power, such as in the employment context, consent is suspicious.

§3. PURPOSE

239. The right to be informed means that the database owner should inform the subject of the intended purpose (section 11(1)), but it does not limit the purpose for which the data is collected.[276] At least in standard contracts, the purpose should be stated in a clear manner.[277]

240. However, once the purpose is stated, the database owner is tied to that particular purpose in the sense that deviating from such purpose constitutes a civil tort. Section 2(9) lists, as one of the privacy torts, the purpose limitation principle: 'using, or passing on to another, information on a person's private affairs otherwise than for the purpose for which it was given' is a violation of privacy. In addition, section 8(b) repeats this principle, regarding databases: 'A person shall not use information in a database that requires registration under this section except for the purpose for which the database was established.' Thus, the purpose stated in the

273. MP (Jerusalem, Standard Contract Court) 7166/99 *D.B.S. Satellite Services (1998) Ltd. v. The Attorney General* (2001), paras 16, 24.
274. M. Birnhack, *Private Space*, *supra* n. 174, 100; and *see, e.g.*, LDA (National Labour Court) 90/08 *Issakov-Inbar v. State of Israel – Commissioner of Law for Women's Work* (2011), para. 28.
275. The PP Authority has expressed a similar view. *See* Database Registrar Guidelines, 2/2012, *The Scope of the Privacy Protection Act Regarding Employment Sorting Processes* (2012), ss 2.3–2.5.
276. *D.B.S.*, at para. 16.
277. *Ibid.*, at para. 22.

notice under section 11(2) is likely to be the baseline purpose for assessing the purpose limitation principle under section 2(9) as well as, depending on the granularity of the notification, under section 8(b).

§4. Form

241. The PPA does not address the form in which the information should be provided,[278] nor does it refer to whether the correlative consent should be in the form of opt-in or opt-out.[279] Other laws may supplement this, for example, the Consumer Protection Act, 1981, which prohibits misleading consumers. General legal principles such as the bona fide principle, which pervades Israeli law, may also come into play. However, there is no direct case law on the matter.

242. In specific cases, the right to be informed is more detailed, as in the health context. Section 13 of the Patients' Rights Act, 1996 instructs that medical treatment is conditioned on receiving the patient's informed consent. The information to be conveyed should be the sufficient information needed in a reasonable manner to make a decision (section 13(b)).

278. *Ibid.*, at paras 18–19 (the court was aware of the fact that users hardly read standard form contracts but pointed to the absence of particular form requirements in the PPA. The court ordered that the information regarding personal data should be emphasized).
279. There are such references in the case of spam. *See* discussion in Part I, Ch. 3.

Chapter 2. Right of Access

§1. Scope

243. The PPA contains an explicit right of access, with accompanying procedural rules. There are some limitations on the exercising right in the case of security agencies.

244. Section 13(a) states:

> Every person is entitled to inspect, either himself or through a representative authorized by him in writing or his guardian, any information about him kept in a database.

245. The right of access can be performed only by the data subject or by an authorized representative.[280] When a person asked for access to CCTV video of other people, the court refused.[281] However, a court (on appeal) ordered an e-scooter rental company to reveal information about a user who allegedly damaged plaintiff's car.[282]

246. Failing to enable access is a criminal offence (section 31A(a)(4)) and a civil tort (section 31B).

247. The PP Authority opined that the right to access covers any format in which the data is kept, including audio and video recordings; and that it applies not only when data is kept under a data subject's name but also in any case in which the data can be related to a person applying reasonable effort.[283] The PP Authority further emphasized the importance of authenticating the identity of the applicant, so to assure that the data provided is handed to the right person. It also emphasized that the data so provided does not contain excessive data that may harm third parties' privacy.

248. In the context of processes for sorting employees, the PP Authority opined that candidates should be entitled to receive the report issued about their performances and abilities by an external evaluation institution; that a general waiver of the access right is void, but specific waivers may be legitimate, such as the sorting

280. Accordingly, when a son asked for data about his father's television service account, without presenting such authorization, the court rejected his request. *See* SC (Jerusalem, Magistrate) 16573-08-12 *Gabay v. Hot, Cable Communications Ltd.* (2013).
281. CC (Haifa, Magistrate) 68953-11-19 *Nagler v. Ness* (2020).
282. CC (Tel Aviv, District) 8720-06-22 *Cohen v. Wind Tel Aviv (Bikey) Ltd.* (2022).
283. Privacy Protection Authority, Instruction 1/2017, The Scope of the Privacy Protection Act regarding the Right to Access Sound Recording, Video Recording, and Additional Digital Data (2017) [Hebrew].

agency's trade secrets.[284] Courts were reluctant, however, to allow access to interviewers' assessments of the job applicants and other internal documents.[285]

§2. Procedures

249. The PPA continues with instructing that the database owner (the term used in the PPA) should enable access in Hebrew, Arabic, or English (section 13(b)).

250. Further conditions for the exercise of the right, including payment, are set in regulations, per section 13(d). Such regulations were issued in 1981.[286] They require that an application to access personal data be in writing, according to a form contained therein (section 1); that the access should be available within thirty days of receiving the application (section 2(a)) and subject to the data subject not mutilating the original documents (section 3). The regulations set a fee of 20 [Old] Shekels, which are equivalent to NIS 0.02 (section 6). The sum was never updated.

§3. Refusal

251. The regulations stipulate that in case the database owner or its holder refuses to allow access, they should inform the applicant within twenty-one days (section 5(a)), and that not responding is to be considered a refusal (section 5(b)).

252. A data subject may contest a database owner's refusal to enable access, by submitting an appeal to a Magistrate Court[287] within thirty days (section 15 of the PPA, section 8 of the Regulations).[288]

§4. Exceptions

253. There are some exceptions to the right of access: first, the database owner may refuse to hand medical or psychological data to the data subject, if he believes the data may cause severe harm to the physical or mental state of the applicants (section 13(c)). In such a case, the data can be handed to a doctor or psychologist

284. Privacy Protection Authority, Instruction 2/2012 The Scope of the Privacy Protection Act Regarding Employment Sorting Processes (2012). The Authority then clarified that the instruction had immediate applicability.
285. CC (Tel Aviv, Magistrate) 52168-02-18 *Alster v. Pioneer Research & Development Ltd.* (2018).
286. Privacy Protection Regulations (Conditions for Accessing Data and Procedures for Appeal on a Refusal to Allow Access), 1981.
287. When plaintiff submitted an appeal to a Small Claims court rather than to the Magistrate Court, the appeal was dismissed. *See* SC (Tel Aviv) 30935-12-15 *Rozenthal v. Erez* (2017).
288. When plaintiff raised this point only in a broader lawsuit against aptitude tests business, the court dismissed this claim. *See* CC (Tel Aviv, District) 10208/05 *Doe v. Pilat (Israel) Ltd.* (2010), para. 47.

on behalf of the data subject. A Family Court ruled that a sister of a legally incompetent person should be able to access financial reports submitted by the legal custodian, an association who sheltered the person. The court found that the best interest of the person was paramount, and in the circumstances, overcame his privacy.[289]

254. A second exception clarifies that the right to access does not permit the breach of a privilege prescribed by law, unless the data subject is the beneficiary of the privilege (section 13(c1)).

255. A third exception exempts certain public authorities from the duty to comply with the request: A security agency, which includes Israel Police, IDF, ISA, Mossad (Israel's Secret Intelligence Service), and the Witness Protection Authority (sections 13(e)(1), 19(c)), as well as the Prison Authority (section 13(e)(1A)), the Tax Authority (section 13(e)(2)),[290] a database of an investigative body – per a declaration by the Minister of Justice (section 13(e)(5)), and a database containing reports made according to the Prohibition of Money Laundering Act, 2000 (section 13(e)(6), referring to section 28 of the said Act).

256. Fourth and related, are exemptions for national security and foreign affairs issues. Section 13(e)(3) contains a general such exception. In addition, the Minister of Justice may determine, after consulting the Minister of Defence or the Minister of Foreign Affairs and with the approval of a Knesset committee, that a database contains data that should not be disclosed, for national security or foreign relations reasons (section 13(e)(4)). A data subject may access unclassified data pertaining to him or her. Such an Order was issued by way of regulations in 1987, adding military industries to the list of exempt bodies.[291]

§5. Criminal Records

257. A special legal regime regulates criminal records. The Criminal Data and Rehabilitation Act, 2019, which entered into force in 2022, replaced a 1981 Act. The Act regulates the collection, retention, and access to such data. The Act has overruled some case law on the matter.

258. According to section 4(a) of the Act, a person has the right to access criminal records about them (with some extensions, in cases of a minor or a person who needs assistance – section 4(b)), but such access is limited to reviewing the data on the police premises, on screen, and prohibits making a copy thereof (section 4(c)), with one exception – providing a print-off to the data subject's attorney for the sole

289. FCt (Tel Aviv, Family Court) 4940/00 *A.Y. v. The Public Trustee* (2002).

290. A district court pointed to this exemption, but then turned to tax laws, and interpreted them so that the Tax Authority was ordered to hand the tax payer her own data. *See* OM (Tel Aviv, District) 1054/00 *Ronen v. Tax Authority* (2000).

291. Privacy Protection Regulations (Determining Databases that Contain Data not to be Revealed), 1987.

purpose of representing the subject in a criminal matter in a court or tribunal (section 4(d)). The Act then lists bodies who are entitled to receive criminal records for the purpose of fulfilling their official roles, subject to various conditions, e.g., the Mossad, may receive such data (section 10(a)(5)).

259. The Act prohibits any other person from demanding that a data subject provides their criminal record, directly or indirectly – e.g., by way of an affidavit to this effect. The Act states that the data subject's consent is irrelevant, and does not render the demand lawful (section 3(b)). Demanding a person to hand their criminal records, directly or indirectly is an offence, with a punishment of up to a year imprisonment, and when done in the context of employment, the punishment is more severe, up to two years (section 42(a)).

260. Prior law permitted broader rights of access, which have been misused by third parties, to obtain personal data:[292] In 1996, the Supreme Court ruled that a person's right to access their criminal record included the right to receive a print-off.[293] An unintended consequence of this ruling was that third parties, especially employers, demanded candidates to provide them with a copy of their criminal record (which may have been null). The Knesset responded in 2007 by amending the Act, prohibiting one from obtaining directly or indirectly the criminal records about another person. Nevertheless, employers bypassed this prohibition by demanding candidates to sign an affidavit regarding their criminal record. The Supreme Court approved this practice, subject to various considerations.[294] The 2019 Act, adopting the recommendations of an expert committee, blocked this route as well, as explained above.

---

292. For discussion, *see* MCrP 1408/14 *Doe v. State of Israel* (2014).
293. HCJ 7256/95 *Fischler v. Police Inspector General*, 50(5) PD 1, 13 (1996).
294. CA 8189/11 *Dayan v. Mifal HaPais*, (2013). A rehearing was granted, but plaintiff then withdrew his appeal. *See* ACH 1840/13 *Dayan v. Mifal HaPais* (2013).

Chapter 3. Rights of Rectification

261. The PPA contains the right to rectification in section 14, when the data 'is not correct, not complete, not clear or not up to date' (section 14(a)).

262. The Privacy Protection Regulations (Conditions for Accessing Data and Procedures for Appeal on a Refusal to Allow Access), 1981 instruct that in the case that the rectification request is approved, the database owner should inform the data subject, and whomever has received the data in the three-year period preceding that time (section 7(a)).

263. A database owner that refuses to rectify the data should inform the data subject (section 14(c)), within thirty days (section 7(b)). Ignoring a request to rectify incorrect data is considered a refusal (section 7(c)). A data subject whose request was denied (or ignored) may appeal to the Magistrate Court (section 8).

264. A database holder is bound by the database owner's consent to rectify the data and by a court order (section 14(d)).

265. Failing to enable rectification is a criminal offence (section 31A(a)(4)) and a civil tort (section 31B).

Chapter 4. Right to Erasure

§1. Introduction

266. Israeli law contains only a partial right to erasure. If a data subject finds out that the data 'is not correct, not complete, not clear or not up to date,' they may ask either that it is amended,[295] or that it is erased (section 14(a)).

§2. Procedures

267. The procedures for approaching the database owner, the meaning of the database owner's inaction and refusal – and the right to approach a court in an appeal, are the same procedures that apply to the right to rectification.[296]

§3. Case Law

268. The PPA's reference to a right to erasure only when the data is incorrect implies that in other cases, the data subject does not have such a right. Accordingly, a district court found that a telecommunication service provider has legitimate business interests as well as tax-related duties in retaining data about users' usage, including the phone numbers, duration of the call, and its timing.[297] While not mentioning section 14, the court denied petitioner's request that data about his calls are deleted once he has paid the bill.

269. The Supreme Court referred to the Court of Justice of the European Union (CJEU) case of *Google v. Agencia Espanola de Proteccion de Datos*, in reviewing an order issued by the Courts' Administration, requiring commercial databases to limit search engine's automatic indexing of legal opinions.[298] While the Court sympathized with the purpose of limiting search options based on a person's name, it concluded that the order disproportionally harmed the commercial service's freedom of occupation. The Court did encourage judges to be aware of the personal data they include in their opinions.[299]

270. Following European law, courts encountered few erasure requests, but absent a statutory anchor, did not recognize a broader right to erasure.[300] In unusual circumstances, a lawyer asked news websites and a search engine to remove data

295. *See* discussion in this part, Ch. 3.
296. *See* Part IV, Ch. 2.
297. CC (Tel Aviv, District) 1994/06 *Liran v. Pelephone Ltd.* (2010).
298. HCJ 5870/14 *Hashavim H.P.S. Business Information Ltd. v. The Courts' Administration* (2015), paras 15, 43. For a critique of the decision, *see* M. Birnhack, *Online Exposure, Legal Exposure: Privacy and the Publication of Court Cases*, 48 Mishpatim 31 (Hebrew U.L. Rev.) (2018) [Hebrew].
299. *Ibid.*, at para. 40. *See also* CA 6356/20 *Doe v. State of Israel – Judge Ronit Bash* (2021), para. 13.
300. *See, e.g.*, CC (Jerusalem, Magistrate) *Tsoknov v. Bezeq International Ltd.* (2017).

about another person, who has the same name. There was no family or any other relationship between the two people; both were lawyers; one of them was convicted in various crimes and was disbarred. The other lawyer was frustrated that search queries prompted results about the first lawyer, thus deterring potential clients. The court found that the original publication was lawful, and that the petitioner had no grounds for erasing the results concerning the other lawyer.[301]

§4. Unlawful Databases

271. An indirect and partial right to erasure may arise when the database at stake is unlawful. At present, all databases that meet certain conditions listed in the PPA (section 8(a)) should be registered with the Database Registrar. Maintaining a database that should be registered, without such registration, is a criminal offence (section 31A(a)(1)). An online newspaper curated reports about a British–Israeli businessperson, including lawsuits submitted to Israeli courts by that person. The businessperson petitioned the court, demanding that the curated webpage is deleted. The district court agreed in part: The webpage contained published judicial opinions, which were open to all, but the lawsuits themselves did not enjoy such publicity.[302] Hence, the court found, the webpage amounted to a 'database', and since it was not registered with the Registrar, the newspaper was ordered to remove it (or, presumably, apply for registration).

§5. Search Engine's Results Display

272. When search results were presented in a misleading manner, which amounted to defamation, a court ordered a search engine to compensate plaintiff.[303] The search engine specialized in Israeli judicial decisions. When searching for plaintiff's name – a lawyer who represented the Israeli bar in disciplinary proceedings against another lawyer – the display suggested that plaintiff was the one who was convicted of disciplinary offences. The court found that this display was the result of the search engine's code, and once notified, its operator should have resolved the matter. Failing to do so harmed plaintiff.

§6. Direct Mailing

273. A special segment of the PPA regulates 'direct mailing' (sections 17C–17I), which is defined as 'contacting a person personally, based on his belonging to a group of the population that is determined by one or more characteristics of persons

301. CA 1139/17 *Miller v. Ha'aretz Publishing Ltd.* (2017).
302. OM (Tel Aviv, District) 9333-12-19 *Soriano v. The Seventh Eye* (2022).
303. CA (Tel Aviv, District) 39345-11-14 *Savir v. Bar-Noy* (2015).

whose names are included in a database' (section 17C). Such direct mailing is different from bulk, unsolicited mail, known as spam, which is regulated in the Communications Act (Telecommunication and Broadcasting), 1982 ('Telecom Act'), and discussed below.[304] Section 17F(b) contains a right to erasure, in the form of an opt-out choice: 'Every person is entitled to demand, in writing, of the owner of the database used for direct mailing that the information relating to him be deleted from the database.' The database owner should act accordingly and notify the data subject (section 17F(d)) within thirty days (section 17F(e)), thereafter, the subject may apply to the Magistrate Court for an order (section 17F(e)). Failing to comply is a civil wrong (section 31B), but is not subject to the statutory damages clause, hence the plaintiff should prove their damages.[305]

274. An entrepreneur established a private 'do not call me' in which he offered data subjects the service of unsubscribing them from mailing lists. He then asked the court for a declaratory remedy, that the service acts as a proxy of its prospective clients, and hence that respondents, financial and communication services, should meet such requests. The PP Authority supported the petition. The district court confirmed that a person has the right to be erased from a database meant for direct mailing, and that a person can be assisted by another for this purpose.[306] However, the petition lacked sufficient details about the particular service, and was dismissed.

§7. Criminal Records

275. A special legal regime regulates criminal records. The Criminal Data and Rehabilitation Act, 2019 which entered into force in 2022, regulates the collection, retention, and access to such data. The Act sets various expungement proceedings (sections 21–23). Expungement does not mean a complete erasure of the criminal record, but a limitation on who may receive such data. The duration of the expungement taking effect is set in the Act, rather than initiated by a data subject.

304. *See* Part I, Ch. 3.

305. CC (Tel Aviv, Magistrate) 57435-04-18 *Bar Ilan v. CalAuto – Financing Service (1998) Ltd.* (2019).

306. OM (Tel Aviv, District) 33104-10-16 *Hershkovitz v. Isracard Ltd.* (2019), para. 19.

Chapter 5. Right to Restriction

276. Israeli law does not contain a general right to restriction. There are several related rules that have a limited, partially similar effect.

277. First, there is a limited right to restrict the usage of personal data in the context of direct mailing.[307] A data subject may demand that a database owner whose database is used for direct mailing (as defined in the PPA, section 17C) limit the delivery of the data to specific people or a kind of people (including corporations) for a limited duration or permanently (section 17F(c)).

278. Second, as discussed above, data subjects have a right to rectification, but the law does not refer to the interim period, of restricting processing while the data controller verifies the accuracy of the data. Presumably, a data subject may ask the Magistrate Court to issue a temporary restraining order, which would seek a similar remedy. At present, no such cases have been filed.

279. Third, where the processing is unlawful – the data subject may complain to the PP Authority, whereas the Database Registrar has the power to suspend the database's registration or delete it from the registry, thus rendering its continued use unlawful (PPA, section 10(f)). The data subject may also petition a court, requesting that it orders the erasure of the database in its entirety. In one case, a court distinguished between lawful segments of the database – a curated webpage referring to plaintiff, regarding judicial opinions in cases he was involved in – and unlawful segments, and ordered the deletion of the latter.[308] In any case, there are few, limited instances in which data subjects have a right to erasure.[309]

280. Fourth, where the data controller no longer needs the personal data, they may delete the database, and in fact, are required to cease using it; otherwise, they would be breaching the purpose limitation duties set in sections 2(9) and 8(b). It seems that the data subject does not have the right to restrict the deletion, although other laws may apply and serve as such a source. At present, there are no cases on this matter.

307. Discussed also in Chs 4 and 6 in this part.
308. OM (Tel Aviv, District) 9333-12-19 *Soriano v. The Seventh Eye* (2022).
309. *See* Ch. 4 of this part.

Chapter 6. Profiling

§1. Introduction

281. Israeli law refers to using and processing personal data kept in databases – defined as electronic collections of data. Unlike the GDPR (Article 4(4)), the PPA does not specifically address the kind of processing, i.e., whether it is automated, nor does the PPA address the purpose of the processing, i.e., whether it is meant to predict data subjects' behaviour.

282. Accordingly, automated and manual processing, regardless of the purpose of the processing, are regulated, but there is no special attention to profiling, other than in the case of direct mailing, discussed below. There is no right in Israeli law 'not to be subject to decisions based solely on automated processing' (GDPR, Article 22). Regular rules apply, namely the right to be informed, right to access, and the limited right to rectification, as well as correlative duties imposed on data processors, as well as confidentiality and data security. Israeli law does not explicitly contain principles such as minimization, explainability, or accountability. It does contain a purpose limitation principle, namely, that data can be used only for the stated purpose (sections 2(9), 8(b)).

§2. Direct Mailing

283. A specific area that the PPA does regulate, that refers to some kinds of profiling, is that of direct mailing, added to the PPA in 1996.[310] While the arrangement's mindset is mostly analogue, it is phrased in a technology-neutral manner. Section 17C defines:

> Direct mailing means contacting a person personally, based on his belonging to a group of the population that is determined by one or more characteristics of persons whose names are included in a database.

284. The legislative explanatory comments of the amendment emphasized that this legal arrangement is not necessarily meant to address harassment, but the non-consensual classification of a person to a particular population segment.[311]

285. A direct mailing database is defined in a broader manner than other databases, as section 17G instructs that this part of the PPA applies not only to 'Data', as defined in section 7, but also to other data relating to the private affairs of a person.

310. *See also* Ch. 4, this part.
311. Quoted in Data Registrar's Instruction 2/2017 Interpretation and Application of the Privacy Protection Act regarding Direct Mailing and Direct Mailing Services (2017).

286. The PPA then requires that a database for direct mailing must be registered as such with the Database Registrar (section 17D); the database owner and manager should document the sources of the data and its recipients (section 17E). A 'direct mailing contact' should state that it is a direct mailing contact, the registration number, information about the right to be deleted from the database, the address of the database owner and the sources of the database (section 17F(a)). The data subject has a right to demand erasure of his or her personal data (section 17F(b)), or restrict the uses of such data (section 17F(c)). Some procedures follow (sections 17F(d), 17F(e)). The PPA further extends these rights to immediate family members (section 17F(f)).

287. A detailed instruction issued by the Database Registrar addresses the sources of a direct mailing database, and submits that when consent for such uses by a direct mailing service (namely, an older version of a data broker) is done via a standard contract, consent should be in the form of opt-in.[312] The Registrar further clarified that an individual contact which is based on the data subject's relationship with the sender, such as sending a customer financial reports, are not considered 'direct mailing'.[313] Another example is of a company which has a database of its customers, for the purpose of providing the service, is not considered direct mailing.[314] The Registrar explained that such contacts are not based on profiling.

312. *Ibid.*, at ss 7–10.
313. *Ibid.*, at s. 13.1.
314. *Ibid.*, at s. 13.2.

Chapter 7. Right to Object

§1. Introduction

288. Israeli law does not contain a right to object to processing of personal data, other than in the few cases where data subjects have the right to erasure of the data.[315]

§2. Withdrawal of Consent

289. Israeli data protection law has only one legal basis for processing: consent (PPA, sections 1, 3, 11(1)). However, the law is silent about withdrawing consent, which could have amounted to a right to object.

290. The Supreme Court addressed the matter in an *obiter dictum*, in a case that dealt with a book published by a man, which despite his claim, was found to contain intimate biographical details about his former lover. The Court found that the woman had not consented to the publication, but nevertheless added comments that imply that a person can withdraw consent, subject, to some extent, to principles of contract law.[316]

291. Lower courts held different opinions on the matter, all in cases that refer to 'traditional privacy torts', rather than direct data protection issues. In one case, a tourist was photographed, with her consent, sunbathing topless at the beach.[317] A few years later, after she immigrated to Israel, her photograph was used again on a cover of a local newspaper, without her permission. The magistrate court considered her initial consent to cover also the second use. In another case, a uniformed soldier participated in the Pride Parade, and his photograph appeared in a national newspaper. The soldier contacted the editors and asked that they do not re-use the photograph again. Nevertheless, the newspaper did use the photograph in other reports regarding LGBT and military service. The magistrate court found that the soldier had the right to withdraw his consent, that his privacy was violated, and awarded the soldier the maximum statutory damages.[318] In a recent case, a magistrate court found that a couple's consent to take intimate photos was based on mutual trust; hence, a person may withdraw her consent at any given moment, resulting in requiring the other party to delete the contents.[319]

315. *See* Ch. 4 above.
316. CA 8954/11 *Doe v. Roe*, 66(3) PD 691, 776–778 (2014), citing, *inter alia*, E. Halm, *Privacy Law* 46 (Perelshtein Genossar Press 2003) [Hebrew]; Birnhack, *Private Space*, *supra* n. 174, at 100–104.
317. CC (Ashdod, Magistrate) 2001/95 *Arieli v. Erev Hadash (Press) Eilat Ltd.* (1998).
318. CC (Jerusalem, Magistrate) 6023/07 *Afriat v. Yediot Acharonot Ltd.* (2008).
319. Crim. C. (Krayot, Magistrate) 19692-07-21 *State of Israel v. Doe* (2022), paras 28, 30. Distributing intimate photos without consent would be both a breach of privacy (PPA, s. 2(4)) and sexual harassment, under the Prevention of Sexual Harassment Act, 1998, s. 3(a)(5A).

Chapter 8. Other Data Subjects' Rights

292. Other than the rights discussed in previous chapters of this Part (right to be informed, right to access data, right to rectify incorrect data, right to erasure if the data is incorrect), data subjects are entitled to rights that correlate to the duties imposed on database owners and database holders. These additional rights are the right to confidentiality and to data security.[320] Violating the duties may give rise to a civil tort (section 31B).

320. For these duties, *see* Part V.

Part V. Duties of Controllers and Processors

Chapter 1. National Rules Regarding Duties of Controllers

§1. Introduction

293. While the PPA acknowledges the concept of data controller (or 'Owner of a Database') as part of the data protection part of the Act, there is no definition of the term, nor does it appear in the privacy tort part of the PPA.[321] Nonetheless, it is clear that the Act acknowledges the concept of data controllers for data protection purposes, and the liability of businesses for potential privacy infringements.

§2. Privacy Infringement Provisions

294. The PPA provides for a main privacy tort – privacy infringement. The actions constituting such privacy infringement may apply to any person, defined in section 4 of the Israeli Interpretation Act, 1981 as both natural persons and legal entities, and thus any business entity performing an action that infringes privacy as per section 2 of the PPA may be liable for such infringement, subject to some exceptions and limitations. In this sense, the PPA treats any entity infringing privacy as liable for its own actions.

§3. Data Protection Provisions

295. As far as the data protection provisions of the PPA are concerned, all the duties included in such provisions apply, first and foremost to controllers of personal data.

296. Such duties include providing the data subject rights,[322] registering databases with the Database Registrar, data security duties.[323]

321. As explained in Part II, Ch. 3.
322. Discussed in Part IV above.
323. Discussed below in Ch. 4 of this part.

297. In some cases, the legal identity of the controller may add additional duties. Thus, public bodies as well as some private bodies which Israeli law deems as 'hybrid' are subject to constitutional norms, for example, the principle of proportionality; as well as employers.

§4. Database Registration

298. The PPA requires data controllers to register their databases (as defined in section 7) in certain circumstances (section 8(c)).

299. A controller must register its database if one of the following conditions are met: The database includes data on 10,000 data subjects or more; the database includes sensitive data (as defined in section 7); data in the databased was not obtained directly from the data subjects or with their consent; the controller is a public body; or the database serves for direct marketing services (as defined in section 17C).

300. The registration duty has several exceptions. First, recall that not any digital collection of data is considered a 'database'.[324] Second, a database should not be registered if it only includes data that has been made publicly available based on a legal authority (section 8(d)).

301. A database registration application should include the identity of the controller, the database manager, and any processors, as well as their contact information, the purposes for which the database was established and for which the data included in it will be used, the types of data included in the database, details on any international data transfers and, if applicable, details on data received from public bodies. The content of the database should not be provided to the Registrar. In practice, the PP Authority established standardized application forms for database registrations, and the registration is also available online.[325] There is no registration fee.

302. The Registrar must review the database registration application within ninety days, and, if no conditional or final refusal have been issued, the database shall be deemed registered following such period (section 10(a)–(b1)). The Registrar has the power to refuse registration if there is a reasonable basis to believe that the data was obtained unlawfully, or that it is meant to serve illegal actions (section 10(a)(1)).[326] The Registrar has the additional power to suspend registration or delete the registration of a database, if the database owner or possessor has violated the PPA or related regulations (section 10(f)).[327]

---

324. *See* discussion in Part II, Chs 2–3.

325. Privacy Protection Authority, Database Registration Application, at https://forms.gov.il/globalData/GetSequence/getHtmlForm.aspx?formType=rishummaagar@justice.gov.il.

326. For such a rare case, *see* CA 439/88 *Database Registrar v. Ventura*, 48(3) PD 808 (1994).

327. Appeals on the Registrar's decisions are submitted to the District Court, residing as an Administrative Court. *See* Administrative Courts Act, 2000, Appendix 1, s. 28.

303. Failing to comply with the duty to register a database is sanctionable as a criminal strict liability offence (section 31A(a)(1)), by administrative fines of up to NIS 10,000,[328] and constitutes a civil wrong (section 31B).

304. There has been recurring criticism of the registration duty, e.g., by the 2007 Schoffman Committee,[329] by the State Comptroller,[330] as well as bills to limit the duty,[331] but so far, the law has not been changed.

328. Administrative Offences Regulations (Administrative Fine – Protection of Privacy), 2004.
329. Committee for Reviewing Legislation in the Area of Databases (J. Schoffman, Chair, Jerusalem 2007). One of the authors (Birnhack) was a member of the committee.
330. State Comptroller and Ombudsman of Israel, 64-3 Annual Report: Registration of Databases in Israel (2014).
331. Privacy Protection Bill (Amendment No. 14), 2022.

Chapter 2. National Rules Regarding Joint Controllers

305. The PPA does not explicitly acknowledge the concept of joint controllers. However, given that violations of both the privacy tort part and the data protection part of the PPA are considered civil torts, as per sections 4 and 31B of the PPA, general tort law principles apply to such provisions.

306. The Israeli Torts Ordinance [New Version] provides for a general concept of joint tortfeasors. Section 11 of the Ordinance states that 'When each or more persons is liable under the provisions of this Ordinance for any act and such act constitutes a civil wrong, such persons shall be jointly liable as joint civil wrong doers for such act and may be sued therefor jointly or severally.'

307. In addition, section 12 of the Torts Ordinance acknowledges the concept of aiding and abetting, and states that 'for the purpose of this Ordinance, any person who joins or aids in, authorizes, counsels, commands, procures or ratifies any act done or to be done, or any omission made or to be made, by any other person shall be liable for such act or omission.'

308. While courts have not yet applied these principles to privacy infringements or data protection violations under the PPA, in other fields of law these principles served courts to create substantive new doctrines to treat unforeseen circumstances at the backdrop of outdated laws, especially in the technological context. For example, courts developed the patent and copyright doctrine of contributory infringement, based on section 12 of the Torts Ordinance.[332] It is thus possible that, in suitable circumstances, courts will acknowledge joint controllership, and, consequently, the liability of one controller to the acts of another controller acting in concert, for violations of the PPA.

332. In Patents: CA 1636/98 *Rav Bariach Ltd. v. Havshush Auto Accessories Trading House (1987) Ltd.*, 55(5) PD 337 (2001); in copyright: CA 8485/08 *Premier League v. Israel Sports Betting Council* (2010); CA 5977/07 *The Hebrew University v. Schocken Publishing House Ltd.*, 64(3) PD 740 (2011); CA 5097/11 *Telran Communications, Ltd. v. Charlton, Ltd.* (2013).

Chapter 3. National Rules with Regard to Processors

§1. Definition and Scope

309. The concept of data processor is explicitly acknowledged and defined in the PPA. The term 'processor' is defined as 'a person who has a database in his possession permanently and is permitted to use it'.[333] This is a narrow conception of a data processor as it is limited to entities having possession over databases permanently. The definition does not address new situations, such as a third party that has remote access to a database or, third parties that have access or possession of either partial segments of databases, or full databases but for a limited duration of time. Courts have not yet addressed these issues

§2. Duties and Liabilities

310. The PPA provides for a limited set of direct duties and liabilities of processors. First, processors have a duty, in certain circumstances, to support controllers with responding to data access requests under section 13A, as well as rectification requests under section 14 of the PPA.

311. Second, processors are under direct confidentiality obligations with respect to any personal data processed in such capacity (section 16), and are liable for the data security of the personal data processed (section 17). In this regard, the DataSec Regulations apply, almost equally, to controllers and processors, and processors must directly comply with such Regulations with respect to their processing of personal data.

312. Third, processors processing personal data on behalf of various controllers must separate between such processing activities (section 17A(a)), and, if more than five databases (as defined in the PPA) are processed, processors must appoint a data security manager and report their data processing activities to the Database Registrar (who is the Head of the PP Authority) annually (section 17A(b)).

§3. Controller–Processor Engagements

313. While the PPA itself does not address the relationship between controllers and processors, the DataSec Regulations as well as guidelines issued by the PP Authority include provisions mandating certain contractual provisions in engagements between controllers and processors.

333. *See* Part II, Ch. 3.

314. The Privacy Protection Authority Guidelines from 2011 set forth a list of requirements that a controller must meet before outsourcing personal data processing activities to a third party.[334] These include preliminary assessments as to the legality of the outsourcing itself, the scope of data to be outsourced and the method of outsourcing as well as the identity and proficiency of the third party providing the outsourcing services.

315. In addition, the Guidelines require controller to include contractual provisions in its engagement with the processor to ensure compliance with the PPA and its underlying regulations, including purpose limitation provisions, mechanisms ensuring assistance with data subject rights, information security provisions, audit and inspection provisions allowing the controller to meaningfully supervise the activities of the processor, and data deletion obligations upon request of the controller or at the end of the services.

316. Section 15 of the DataSec Regulations further requires controllers to consider and assess data security risks and potential impact of allowing processors access to their databases, as well as mandatory contractual provisions to be included in a controller–processor agreement. These include: (i) The data that the processor is allowed to process and the allowed use purposes; (ii) The data systems the processor is allowed to access; (iii) The type of processing or activities the processor is allowed to conduct; (iv) The term of the engagement and mechanisms to return or delete the personal data upon expiration; (v) The manner in which the processor would comply with the provisions of the DataSec Regulations; (vi) The duty of the processor to sign any permitted representatives on confidentiality and information security undertakings; (vii) Imposing all of the above duties on any sub-processors; and (viii) The processor's duty to report, at least once annually, in the manner in which it complies with the DataSec Regulations and the agreement, and notify the controller of any personal data breach.

334. Database Registrar Guideline, 1/2011, *Use of Data Regarding the Imposition of Foreclosure* (2011).

Chapter 4. Security Obligations

§1. Introduction

317. Section 17 of the PPA sets forth that controllers, processors, and database managers are liable for the data security of the databases. Section 7 of the PPA defines 'data security' as 'protection of the integrity of the data, or protection of the data from being exposed, used or copied, without lawful permission.' The DataSec Regulations derive from these provisions and set forth a detailed list of technical and organizational requirements from controllers and processors as discussed below.

318. Many of the provisions in the DataSec Regulations are drafted in a relatively open manner, using standards such as 'reasonableness', 'as appropriate', 'to the extent possible', 'adequate', etc. This legislative technique allows flexibility and adopting general principles to specific technologies and business models, and leaves room for judicial or regulatory interpretation.

§2. Modular Applicability

319. Given that the DataSec Regulations apply to any controller or processor of personal data, regardless of sector, volume, or sensitivity of the personal data processed, they include modular applicability of certain provisions according to the security level of the applicable database. The regulations acknowledge three security levels: basic security level, medium security level, and high security level.

320. Medium security level databases are those that include medical data, data on the private affairs of a person, data on an individual's political opinions or religious beliefs, biometric data, economic data such as the data subject's assets, debts or consumption habits, as well as databases designated for Direct Mailing.[335] Databases of public bodies or of controllers who are data brokers are subject to a medium security level regardless of the types of data or number of access permissions.[336]

321. Databases which include data on employees or vendors only, or allows access permissions to up to ten individuals, remain in basic level of security.[337]

322. High security level databases are those that meet the medium security level criteria but also include either data on 100,000 or more individuals or more than 100 access permissions.[338]

335. DataSec Regulations, Annex 1, item 1(3).
336. *Ibid.*, items 1(1)–(2).
337. *Ibid.*, item 2.
338. DataSec Regulations, Annex 2.

§3. Record of Processing Activities

323. Section 2 of the DataSec Regulations requires controllers to maintain a record of processing activities including the following information: (i) General description of the collection and use activities of the data; (ii) Description of the use purposes of the data; (iii) The types of data included in the database; details on the transfer of data outside of Israel, the purpose of such transfers, the destination country, the manner of transfer and the identity of the transferee; (iv) Processing activities by processors; (v) The main data security risks and their mitigation measures; (vi) The name of the database Managers, the processors and the Security Supervisor, if applicable.

324. Controllers must review and update the record of processing annually or upon material changes or data breaches and must consider whether excessive data is retained.[339]

§4. Data Security Policy

325. The DataSec Regulations require controllers and processors to formulate and adopt a data security policy that is adequate to the nature of processing of personal data, and are binding upon all access holders. The policy must address physical security, access control and permissions, the measures of data security employed and their manner of operation, acceptable use guidelines to access holders, an analysis of the risks that apply to the database, the risk methodology and mitigation steps including encryption, data breach mitigation and response procedures, and the use of portable media.

326. Controllers and processors of medium and high security level databases must also address authentication and identification measures, monitoring and control over the use of the database, periodic assessments, back-up procedures and secure development of the database and its underlying systems.

327. The policy should be reviewed and updated annually or upon material changes or the introduction of new technological risks.

§5. System Mapping and Risk Assessments

328. The DataSec Regulations require controllers and processor to map all systems used for the operation of a database including infrastructure and hardware, software, network diagrams, and endpoints. Such document should be readily available only on a need-to-know basis.[340]

339. DataSec Regulations, ss 2(b)–(c).
340. DataSec Regulations, s. 5(a).

329. For high security level databases, controllers and processors are required to conduct data security risk assessments and penetration tests once every eighteen months. They should also review the conclusions of such assessments and act to mitigate any deficiencies identified.[341]

§6. Physical Security

330. Controllers and processors must ensure that the infrastructure and hardware systems of the database will be stored in a secured space preventing unauthorized access, given the nature of the processing of personal data.[342]

331. In medium and high security level databases, controllers and processors must undertake measures to control and log the entry and exit from the sites in which such infrastructure and hardware systems are stored. This effectively requires some sort of an automated physical access control system.[343]

§7. Data Security in Human Resources Management

332. Controllers and processors must undertake appropriate measures to ensure that employees who have access to the databases are suitable to receive such access, while taking into account the sensitivity of the data contained in the databases. In addition, they are required to hold training sessions for employees before granting access to the databases.

333. Controllers and processors of medium and high security level databases are required to hold periodic training sessions for their employees – at least once every twenty-four months.

§8. Access Control, Identification and Authentication

334. Controllers and processors must establish role-based access control permissions to the database systems, on a need-to-know basis. These should be documented and updated regularly.[344] Permissions should be revoked upon termination of an employee's role requiring the respective access.[345]

341. DataSec Regulations, ss 5(c)–(d).
342. DataSec Regulations, s. 6(a).
343. DataSec Regulations, s. 6(b).
344. DataSec Regulations, s. 8.
345. DataSec Regulations, s. 9(c).

335. Controllers and processors must also take customary measures to ensure, given the nature of processing, that access is only granted based on the valid access control permissions.[346]

336. In medium and high security level databases the identification of permission holders will be done, to the extent possible, based on two-factor authentication, and the identification system will include a password policy that enforces semi-annual password change, automatic logouts and will treat identification-related errors.[347]

337. In medium and high security level databases, controllers and processors must apply an automatic monitoring and logging system, logging at least the user identity, time and date of the access attempt, the system to which access was attempted, the type and scope of access sought and whether access was granted or denied. These logs should be kept for a period of twenty-four months, and should be backed up and retained in a restorable state together with security logs from other systems required by the Regulations.

§9. Data Breach Management and Notification

338. The DataSec Regulations require that controllers and processors log any event that raises concern for the breach of the data integrity or unauthorized use, to the extent possible in an automated manner.

339. In medium security level databases, annual meetings are required to discuss data security events, and in high security level, on a quarterly basis.

340. The DataSec Regulations require controllers and processors to notify the Database Registrar of any severe security event, and the Registrar may, in adequate circumstances, require them to notify the data subjects directly. The PP Authority has explained that such notification should be immediate and without undue delay from becoming aware of the event.[348]

341. The definition of 'severe security event' is adapted to each security level. For basic security level databases there are no severe security events and thus no breach notification duty. For medium security level databases, notification is required only if a material part of the data in the database was affected in terms of integrity or unauthorized use. For high security level databases, any unauthorized use or breach of integrity of the database should be notified.

---

346. DataSec Regulations, s. 9(a).
347. DataSec Regulations, s. 9(b).
348. The Implementation of the Privacy Protection (Data Protection) Regulations' Guidelines – Information Security Incident Notification to the Privacy Protection Authority (2021).

342. We note that, as discussed in Part II, Chapter 3, that the definition of the term 'data security', both in the PPA and the DataSec Regulations, does not directly address the issue of availability. Given that the term 'use' is defined in broad terms, questions may arise in circumstances where a security incident affected only the availability of a database but not its integrity or unauthorized use, or when there is unauthorized access to a database but it is unclear given the circumstances if the third party used the database.

§10. Communication Security, Secure Development and Portable Media

343. The Regulations require controllers and processors to restrict or prevent the use of portable media given the security level applicable to the database and the nature of processing. Using customary encryption techniques will be considered as reasonable measures to protect data in portable media.[349]

344. Controllers and processors must maintain proper management of the database systems, as customary, separate, to the extent possible, between the database systems and other systems in the organization and maintain ongoing patch management and cease using unsupported systems.

345. Controllers and processors must not connect the database systems to the internet or to public network without employing adequate security measures to prevent unauthorized access or damage to data and systems, and shall ensure that any Information transfers over public networks is encrypted with customary measures. When remote access is available, authentication must be based on two factors.[350]

§11. Exemptions

346. The Database Registrar is authorized to exempt *specific* organizations from all or part of the Regulations. As of December 2022, no such specific exemptions were granted. In addition, the Registrar is authorized, if convinced that other regulations or official standards provide adequate information security measures as required under the DataSec Regulations, to exempt organizations subject to such other regulations or certified under such standards from part or all of the Regulations.[351]

347. The Database Registrar has issued partial exemptions for certain sectors, e.g., organizations subject to data security regulations issued by the Inspector of

349. DataSec Regulations, s. 12.
350. DataSec Regulations, s. 14(b).
351. DataSec Regulations, s. 20(b).

Banks,[352] data security regulations applicable to insurance companies and pension funds,[353] and organizations holding certification under ISO 27001 by the Israeli Standards Institution.[354]

352. Database Registrar Guideline, 1/2018, *Applicability of the Privacy Protection DataSec Regulations, 2017 to Entities Subject to the Provisions of the Supervisor of Banks* (2018).
353. Database Registrar Guideline, 2/2018, *Applicability of the Privacy Protection DataSec Regulations, 2017 to Management and Insurance Companies Subject to the Provisions of the Capital Market, Insurance and Savings Authority* (2018).
354. Database Registrar Guideline 3/2018, *Applicability of the Privacy Protection DataSec Regulations, 2017 to Organizations Certified to the IEC/ISO 27001 Standard* (2018).

Chapter 5. DPO or Similar Functions

§1. Introduction

348. The PPA does not address the function of a DPO and there is no binding legal requirement to appoint one under Israeli law, but for few databases of public bodies. The PPA does provide for two other mandatory functions – Database Manager and Security Supervisor; these roles, however, are not identical to the GDPR's DPO tasks (GDPR, Article 39). The PP Authority issued recommendations on the appointment of a DPO, explaining its approach to the scope of the role and its functions. The National Labour Court recommended the appointment of a privacy trustee in workplaces.

§2. Statutory DPOs

349. The PPA itself does not address the function of a DPO, and Israeli law does not generally require the appointment of such role. However, there are several industry-specific legislations that do require the appointment of DPOs. The Bank of Israel Commissioner must appoint a DPO with respect to its mandatory credit score database.[355] The Minister of Interior Affairs must appoint a DPO with respect to the government-operated biometric database.[356] The Bank of Israel Guidelines require banks and other regulated entities to appoint a compliance position pertaining to privacy and data protection, which, de facto, means a DPO.[357] The Financial Services Inspection Regulations (Pension Advice, Marketing and Clearing System) (Data Security in Central Pension Clearing System), 2012 require any operator of a central clearing system appoint a data protection and security manager (section 3).

§3. Database Manager

350. The PPA requires each controller that is under an obligation to register a database with the Database Registrar, to appoint a Database Manager. A Database Manager is defined as 'an active manager of a body that owns or possesses a database or a person whom the aforesaid manager authorized for this purpose' (section 7). The PPA does not define the roles or proficiency for a Database Manager, and as a matter of fact, this role could be occupied by any employee or contractor of the controller.

351. In terms of responsibilities, the PPA is silent about what a Database Manager is required to do, save that it explicitly provides that a Database Manager is

355. Credit Data Act, 2016, s. 18.

356. Inclusion of the Biometric Identification Measures and Data in Identification Documents and Database Act, 2009, s. 26.

357. Proper Bank Management Guidelines No. 308, Compliance and the Compliance Function in a Bank (2021).

responsible to the data security of the database, and may be liable for failures (sections 16–17). There is no case law considering the roles and responsibilities or the proficiency of a Database Manager.

§4. Security Supervisor

352. Section 17B of the PPA requires controllers and processors who possess five or more databases, as well as public bodies, banks, insurance companies, and credit score companies to appoint a Security Supervisor. The PPA does not address the roles, competence, or proficiency of Security Supervisors, but does set forth that persons who were convicted for offences of moral turpitude or violations of the PPA cannot be appointed as Security Supervisors, and that the Security Supervisor shall be liable to the data security of a database.

353. Section 3 of the DataSec Regulations sets additional requirements pertaining to Security Supervisors, whether appointed due to a binding legal requirement or voluntarily.

354. First, a Security Supervisor should be directly subordinate to the Database Manager or another senior executive directly subordinate to the Database Manager.

355. Second, the Security Supervisor cannot hold another conflicting role in the organization to prevent potential conflict of interests in the managing of the security of databases. This means, for example, that the Security Supervisor cannot generally also be the data technology manager of an organization.

356. Third, the tasks of the Security Supervisor include at least preparing the data security policies and procedures required under the DataSec Regulations, as well as preparing a security work plan and ongoing assessment, and present and confirm the foregoing with the controller (Database owner, in the PPA's terms). If the controller wishes the Security Supervisor to fulfil other functions, these have to be explicitly defined.

357. Last, the controller must allocate adequate resources to allow the Security Supervisor to meet his or her duties set forth above. This, in fact, requires controllers to consider data security requirements in their annual budgets to meet the mandatory requirements of the DataSec Regulations.

§5. Data Protection Officer

358. In 2022, the PP Authority issued recommendations explaining the roles, functions and responsibilities of a DPO for organizations wishing to voluntarily have such a position.[358]

359. The Recommendations explain that the appointment of a DPO is recommended for organizations that are either data-driven, process personal data on a large scale, or create inherent heightened privacy risks. They further explain that this function could be fulfilled either by an internal employee or by an external service provider, depending on the nature of the organization and its maturity level.

360. The PP Authority further clarified that the DPO should have three main roles and responsibilities. First, the DPO should govern the personal data management procedures of an organization, including drafting an internal data protection policy, leading privacy by design efforts, be involved in decision making regarding business processes that involve the processing of personal data, conduct a privacy impact assessment and review the organizations practices for compliance with the PPA and its underlying regulations, be informed of data security assessments, and serve as a point of contact for data protection complaints.

361. Second, the DPO should conduct oversight and audit functions, in which they shall lead an annual compliance audit program, report directly to senior management, at least once annually, supervise the mitigation steps for any compliance gaps identified, and serve as a point of contact for the PP Authority.

362. Third, the DPO should manage the training and awareness efforts of the organization in the field of data protection, vis-à-vis the requirements of the PPA and its underlying regulations.

363. The Authority's recommendations also clarify that the DPO should be a senior position in an organization, part of the management team, and be independent of any other duties or conflicting responsibilities. In terms of proficiency, the Recommendations state that the DPO should have deep understanding of privacy and data protection laws and sufficient technological knowledge, and that he or she should have academic or equivalent legal, accounting, information technology or regulatory accreditation, as well as deep understanding of the business activities of the organization.

358. Privacy Protection Authority Recommendation on the Appointment of a Data Protection Officer, 2022.

§6. Privacy Trustees in Labour Contexts

364. The National Labour Court, in a leading case about privacy in the workplace, has recommended that workplaces appoint a privacy trustee. However, the Court did not outline what would be the functions of such privacy trustees.[359]

359. LA (National) 90/08 *Issakov-Inbar v. State of Israel – The Commissioner for the Women's Labour Law* (2011), 24, following a suggestion in M. Birnhack, *Surveillance at Work: Taylor, Bentham and the Right to Privacy*, 12 Lab., Soc'y & L. 9, 67 (2010) [Hebrew].

Part VI. Codes of Conduct and Certification

365. The PPA does not acknowledge the concept of compliance with codes of conduct or certification as envisaged by section 5 of the GDPR.

366. The PPA does authorize the Minister of Justice to issue regulations regarding operational and ethical rules for owners, possessors, and managers of databases (section 36(3)). As of December 2022, no such rules were issued.

367. In the specific context of the DataSec Regulations, the Database Registrar is authorized, if convinced that other regulations or official standards provide adequate data security measures as required under the DataSec Regulations, to exempt organizations subject to such other regulations or certified under such standards from part or all of the Regulations.[360]

368. Such partial exemptions were issued for organizations holding certification under ISO 27001 by the Israeli Standards Institution,[361] which form some sort of acknowledgement in certification as a method for data protection compliance.

369. Ethical codes of other professionals may be relevant in assessing defences, related to privacy torts. One group of defences contains a prerequisite of acting in good faith (section 18(2)). For some of these defences, the PPA creates a presumption of good faith for those who followed relevant ethical norms (section 20(c)). A leading example is journalists' codes of ethics.[362]

---

360. DataSec Regulations, s. 20(b); *see also* Part V, Ch. 4.
361. Database Registrar Guideline 3/2018, *Applicability of the Privacy Protection DataSec Regulations, 2017 to Organizations Certified to the IEC/ISO 27001 Standard* (2018).
362. *See also* discussion in Part IX, Ch. 1.

Part VII. International Transfers

Chapter 1. General Principles

370. The Privacy Protection Regulations (Transfers of Data to Databases Abroad), 2001 (Data Transfer Regulations), promulgated under the PPA govern the cross-border transfers of personal data originating in Israel. They apply to both controllers and processors not just to the processing of data retained in databases, as defined in the PPA.

371. The Regulations provide that no person may transfer data from databases located in Israel to other countries, unless the law in the recipient country provides the same level of data protection afforded in Israel.[363] This, in principle, follows the same concept promoted in Article 46 of the GDPR.

372. The Data Transfer Regulations provide a list of exemptions for statutorily approved cross-border transfers. Cross-border data transfers are presumed to be permitted in the following circumstances:[364]

(1) where the data subject agreed to the transfer of his/her data;[365]
(2) where it is impossible to obtain the consent of the subject of the data and the transfer is necessary to protect the subject's health;
(3) where the data is transferred to an entity in the control of the transferor and it has secured the adequate protection of the information;
(4) where the data is transferred to a third party who agrees to provide the same level of data protection required under Israeli law;[366]
(5) where the data was released to the public, under lawful authority;
(6) where the transfer of data is necessary to protect public safety;
(7) where the transfer of data is required under Israeli law;

363. Privacy Protection Regulations (Transfers of Data to Databases Abroad), 2001, s. 1.
364. *Ibid.*, s. 2.
365. It is unclear whether a specific consent for a specific transfer is required or if a general consent to a type of transfers and jurisdictions will suffice.
366. Practically, this means that a data transfer agreement between the transferor and transferee could establish a legal basis for the cross-border transfer. There are no pre-approved data transfer agreements.

(8) where the transfer of data is to a country which is (1) a member of The Convention for the Protection of Individuals with regard to Automatic Processing of Personal Data; (2) is allowed to receive data from members of the EU; or (3) the Database Registrar has determined as adequate for such transfers.

373. Although the Data Transfer Regulations generally prohibit onward transfers,[367] in 2022, the PP Authority published a draft opinion in which it stated that as this restriction is not in line with recent technological developments and with the current structure of international economic and trade relations, the PPA would not deem onward transfers as a violation of the Data Transfer Regulations, provided that: (i) the controller granted its written consent to the onward transfer, (ii) the transfer to a third party was lawful, and (iii) an otherwise direct transfer between the controller and such third party would meet one of the conditions listed above.[368]

374. It is noteworthy that according to the Cloud Computing Guidelines issued by the BoI, a banking corporation must not store customer data or data with cloud services outside Israel unless such cloud service provider meets the obligations of the GDPR.[369]

367. *Ibid.*, s. 3.
368. Privacy Protection Authority, Legal Opinion, *Interpretation of S. 3 of the Privacy Protection Regulations (Transfers of Data to Databases Abroad), 2001* (January 2022).
369. Proper Bank Management Guidelines, Cloud Computing (2022).

Chapter 2. Transfers in the Context of International Agreements

375. There is no specific treatment of personal data transfers in the context of international agreements in Israel, such as mutual assistance treaties and similar mechanisms. However, given that section 2(7) of the Data Transfer Regulations explicitly approves the transfer of data from databases where such transfer is required under applicable law, if an implementation act for any such treaty or international agreement requires the transfer of personal data, such transfer would generally be lawful.

Part VIII. Enforcement

Chapter 1. Supervisory Authorities

376. Israel has one supervisory authority tasked directly with enforcing (some) privacy matters, the PP Authority. The Authority was established in 2006 under the name ILITA, by integrating several statutory powers, regarding the PPA, as well as the Digital Signature Act, 2001 and the Credit Data Services Act, 2002 (which was replaced by the Credit Data Act, 2016). In 2017, ILITA was renamed as the PP Authority. Other regulators may have some powers to regulate data protection issues as part of regulating the relevant industry, such as in the communication and financial services. We focus on the PP Authority.

377. The PP Authority in its current form is an administrative unit within the Ministry of Justice.[370] The Authority does not have an independent budget; rather, its budget is part of the Ministry's general budget.

378. The PPA does not mention the Authority,[371] and the statutory powers are designated to the Database Registrar, who directs the Authority.

379. The role of the Database Registrar was created in the 1980s, following the enactment of the PPA. The Registrar's roles and powers were then expanded in 1996, with minor amendments later on. Various bills to further enhance the powers and consolidate the status of the Registrar or of the PP Authority have not been successful so far.

380. The PPA mentions in passing the Public Council for the Protection of Privacy (section 10A) stating that the Council should comment on the Database Registrar's annual report, submitted to the Knesset. The PPA says nothing more of this Council, which is loosely regulated in internal rules issued by the Minister of Justice. In practice, the Council is composed of several non-governmental experts, and provides some non-binding advice to the Authority.

---

370. *See* https://www.gov.il/en/departments/the_privacy_protection_authority/govil-landing-page.
371. The Authority was mentioned once in legislation, in an Act that has now expired: the Authorizing the General Security Service to Assist in the National Effort to Minimize the Spread of the New Covid Virus and Promoting the Use of Civil Contact Tracing Technologies (Temporary) Act, 2020. Section 12(a) authorized the PP Authority to submit an opinion to a ministerial cabinet, for the purpose of a governmental decision about operating the ISA surveillance tools for COVID-related contact tracing. For discussion of this surveillance, *see* Part I, Ch. 1.

Chapter 2. Composition

381. The PP Authority is headed by the Database Registrar. The Registrar is appointed by the government (PPA, section 7), and should meet the qualifications required to be appointed to a Magistrate Judge (section 7).

382. The PPA is silent about the term of the Registrar. A 2009 government decision set the term to six years, along various other gate-keeping regulators whose independence was deemed especially important.[372] A 2022 government decision has reaffirmed this decision, and determined that the PP Authority is independent from the Ministry of Justice in its decision making processes and its budget.[373]

383. The PP Authority is composed of several departments: A regulation and legal department; an enforcement department, innovation and policy development department, and strategic alliances department.[374] The enforcement department is tasked with criminal investigations, inspection and administrative investigations, audits, intelligence, and computer forensics.[375]

384. At present, the Authority has a staff of sixty employees.[376]

372. Government Decision (No. 4470) List of High Ranking Positions in the State Service subject to the Arrangement regarding the Position's Term (2009), at https://www.gov.il/he/departments/policies/2009_des4470 [Hebrew].
373. Government Decision (No. 1890) Independence of the Privacy Protection Authority (2022), at https://www.gov.il/he/departments/policies/dec1890-2022 [Hebrew].
374. *See* https://www.gov.il/BlobFolder/generalpage/organizational_structure_ilita/en/RAMUT_EN_0.pdf.
375. *Ibid.*
376. Privacy Protection Authority, Annual Report for the Year 2021, at 7 (2022).

Chapter 3. Competence, Tasks and Powers

385. The PPA empowers the Database Registrar to supervise compliance with the Act (section 10(c)). The Registrar has two main tasks: Registration of databases and enforcement.

386. The PPA requires that databases (as defined in section 7) that meet at least one of the conditions set therein (section 8(c)) should be registered (section 8(a)), or else, it would be a criminal offence to manage or possess such a database (section 31A(a)(1)). The registration is of the database, and does not include providing the Registrar with the contents of the database. The Registrar has the power to refuse registration if he has a reasonable basis to that the data was obtained unlawfully, or that it is meant to serve illegal actions (section 10(a)(a)).[377] The Registrar has the additional power to suspend registration or delete a database, if the database owner or possessor has violated the PPA or related regulations (section 10(f)).[378]

387. There has been recurring criticism of the registration duty, e.g., by the 2007 Schoffman Committee,[379] by the State Comptroller,[380] as well as bills to limit the duty,[381] but so far, the law has not been changed.

388. The PPA authorizes the Minister of Justice to establish an enforcement unit (section 10(d)), directed by the Registrar (section 10(e)), composed of professional inspectors, trained in computers and data security, and that the Police has not object to their appointment (section 10(e)).

389. An inspector has the power to require any person to provide information and documents about a database without a warrant (section 10(e1)(1)), and to enter a place where the inspector has a reasonable reason to believe that it hosts a database, to search the premises, and seize objects, including computers and computer content without a warrant, all in order to enforce the PPA and prevent offences (section 10(e1)(2)). Exercising the search and seizure powers in residential places only requires a judicial warrant (section 10(e1)(3)).

390. In practice, enforcement activities are directed at both public bodies such as municipalities and political parties, and privacy corporations such as financial, health, and communication service providers.[382] According to its own annual report, in 2021 the Authority engaged in 101 cases: 29 cases about using data for uses that exceed the purpose for which it were collected, data collection without consent and

377. *See* CA 439/88 *Database Registrar v. Ventura*, 48(3) PD 808 (1994).
378. Appeals on the Registrar's decisions are submitted to the District Court, residing as an Administrative Court. *See* Administrative Courts Act, 2000, Appendix 1, s. 28.
379. Committee for Reviewing Legislation in the Area of Databases (J. Schoffman, Chair, Jerusalem 2007). One of the authors (Birnhack) was a member of the committee.
380. State Comptroller and Ombudsman of Israel, 64-3 Annual Report: Registration of Databases in Israel (2014).
381. Privacy Protection Bill (Amendment No. 14), 2022.
382. Privacy Protection Authority, Annual Report, at 23–25.

refusal to enable access; 32 cases of data security; 5 criminal cases (2 convictions, 2 sentences, one of new charges). Other enforcement cases dealt with the Authority's other power, not related to the PPA.[383] The unit has also performed 96 audits, for 32 data security breaches and 29 violations of the purpose limitation principle, and the remaining for non-privacy cases.[384]

391. As of 2018, the Authority conducts industry-wide audits, which is based on surveys of relevant players in each examined sector. For example, in 2021, the Authority examined four sectors: Human power agencies, cosmetic clinics, retail shops in the food and fuel sectors, and professional pension funds.[385]

392. The PPA does not have an independent standing in courts, and the Attorney General's office represents its view and litigates its cases in court. Once the Government makes a decision on a matter, the Authority is bound by the governmental position, and may not advocate for a different approach, for example in Knesset committees.

393. The PPA is silent about the Registrar's policy powers. However, ILITA and now the PP Authority have issued various instructions, opinions, and recommendations over the years, regarding various personal data-related issues. An administrative court discussed the Registrar's instruction to insurance companies prohibiting the use of data provided to them for foreclosures, for the separate purpose of considering an insurance policy.[386] The insurance company argued that the Registrar lacked the authority to issue such instructions. The court referred to section 10(c) of the PPA, which instructs that 'The Registrar shall supervise compliance with the provisions of this Law and the regulations thereunder,' and to specific Registrar's powers, and concluded that the Registrar was authorized to issue such instructions, which reflect his interpretation of the law.[387] The court emphasized that such instructions should meet the reasonability test, and be a plausible interpretation of the law.

394. The Registrar has an additional task, to prepare an annual report to be submitted to the Knesset Committee on Constitution and Law (section 10A). The report should be accompanied along the comments of the Public Council for the Protection of Privacy.

395. In additional to its statutory tasks, the Authority is involved in internal governmental processes meant to promote updated legislation (at present, to no avail), and discussions with the EU regarding Israel's adequacy status, which is currently under review, per the GDPR. The Authority also publishes various instructions –

383. *Ibid.*, at 20.
384. *Ibid.*, at 21.
385. *Ibid.*, at 29.
386. AA (Tel Aviv, District) 24867-02-11 *IDI Insurance Co. Ltd. v. Database Registrar* (2012). An appeal to the Supreme Court was withdrawn, with the Court noting that it agrees with the District court's opinion. AA 7043/12 *IDI Insurance Co. Ltd. v. Database Registrar* (2014).
387. *Ibid.*, at para. 3.

deemed to reflect its interpretation of the law, and non-binding guidelines, such as guidelines for performing a data protection impact assessment,[388] or guidelines regarding long distance exams in higher education institutions during COVID.[389]

388. *See* https://www.gov.il/BlobFolder/rfp/dpia_guide_draft/he/privacy_survay_new.pdf [Hebrew].
389. https://www.gov.il/BlobFolder/reports/privacy_academic_studies_corona/he/academic_exam.pdf [Hebrew].

Chapter 4. Remedies

§1. Introduction

396. Given that the privacy and data protection provisions in the PPA are classified as civil wrongs (sections 4, 31B), violation of such provisions provides the victims the key remedies provided under general tort law in Israel, namely injunctive relief and damages. As for damages, general tort law in Israel acknowledged both pecuniary and non-pecuniary damages that should be proven, and the PPA also provides for statutory damages in certain circumstances.

§2. Injunctive Relief

397. Sections 71–72 of the Torts Ordinance [New Version] provide that any civil court can issue injunctions with respect to wrongs committed. This is a general authorization to courts to provide injunctive relief for torts-related violations.[390]

398. In addition, section 29(a) of the PPA provides that:

> In addition to any penalty and other relief, the court may, in a criminal or civil proceeding for infringement due to a violation of a provision of this law, order – (1) prohibition of the distribution of copies, or confiscation, of the infringing matter; a confiscation order under this paragraph is effective against any person who has such material in his possession for sale, distribution or storage, also if he is not a party to the proceeding; where the court orders confiscation, it shall direct how the confiscated copies shall be disposed of; (2) publication of the whole or part of the judgment; the publication shall be made at the expense of the accused or defendant, in the place and in the dimensions and manner prescribed by the court; (3) surrender of the infringing matter to the injured party; (4) destruction of information unlawfully received, or prohibition of use of the aforesaid information or of excess information as defined in section 23E, or any other order in respect of the information.

399. These provisions allow courts with a flexible framework for issuing injunctive orders with respect to privacy and data protection violations. We note that the various injunctive orders are not mandatory, rather they are discretional. Courts have not yet explained what would be the factors considered for deciding whether to issue such injunctions in civil or criminal proceedings. Also, while in many cases such injunctions were issued in privacy tort-related cases, they are also available for data protection infringements.[391] While these injunctions are perceived as permanent injunctions which are an independent remedy that could be sought by plaintiffs in a privacy or data protection infringement proceeding, we note that at least one

390. Crim. A. 2/73 *Selah v. State of Israel*, 28(2) PD 371 (1974).

391. *See, e.g.*, MCP (Tel Aviv, District) 22526/06 *Israel Bar Association v. Ayalon Insurance Company Ltd.* (2006).

court accepted the Attorney General's *ex parte* petition for issuing an order restricting dissemination of personal data leaked in a high-profile data breach, without any substantive legal proceeding and with the order being issued against any person in the possession of such personal data.[392]

§3. Damages

400. Section 76 of the Torts Ordinance allows any victim of a civil wrong to seek damages that are caused by the wrong. This equally applies to violations of the privacy torts and data protection provisions of the PPA, and thus, plaintiffs can seek and prove their damages from such violations.

401. Israeli tort law generally acknowledges various types of damages. The primary type of damages are pecuniary damages that result from the wrong.[393] On top of the general causation requirement under tort law, when pure economic damage is concerned courts are reluctant to award damages except for extraordinary circumstances.[394] In privacy and data protection contexts, pecuniary damages are, in most cases, not easy to prove, save for data breach incidents that relate to financial data or credentials that could lead to actual pecuniary losses.

402. Israeli tort law also acknowledges non-pecuniary damages. These include various sub-categories. The first is damages for mental damages which is generally aims at quantifying the harms a victim suffered due to mental illness or disorder caused by the wrong.[395] The second is damages for pain and suffering harm, which is aimed at the quantification of the physical or mental distress caused by the wrong.[396] This category is often alleged by plaintiffs in cases of data breaches including sensitive data or misuse of data in the core of their privacy right.[397] The third is harm to autonomy. This is a relatively new sub-category of non-pecuniary damages developed in the field of medical treatment, which focuses on the harm caused to a person by negating his or her right to make autonomous decisions.[398] The same concept has been extended, in specific circumstances, to consumer-related claims pertaining to unwanted substances included in consumer products.[399] Courts are, however, generally reluctant to award damages for consumer-related harms to autonomy and require a relatively high threshold of proving harms to the hard-core of a person's autonomy which led to 'severe feelings' or 'disgust'.[400]

---

392. *See* case 6485-11-21 (Central District) *In re CyberServe Internet & Communications Ltd.* (3 Nov. 2021).
393. LCA 5237/06 *Israel's Administration of the Courts v. Mansour* (2008).
394. OM 106/54 *Weinstein v. Kadima Water Supply Association Ltd.*, 8 PD 1317 (1954); CA 4493/05 *Yerushalmi v. Polaris Importing Tools Ltd.*, 62(2) PD 1, 19–20 (2007).
395. CA 754/05 *Levi v. Shaare Zedek Medical Center*, 62(2) PD 218 (2007).
396. CA 773/81 *Freilich Estate v. State of Israel*, 36(4) PD 816 (1982).
397. Class A. (Be'er Sheva, District) 41837-09-16 *Doe v. Daka90 Ltd.* (2019).
398. CA 2781/93 *Da'aka v. Carmel Hospital*, 54(4) PD 526 (1999).
399. CA 1338/97 *Tnuva Cooperative Ltd. v. Raabi*, 54(4) PD 673 (2003).
400. CA 10085/08 *Tnuva Cooperative Ltd. v. Raabi Estate* (2011).

403. Due to difficulties in proving harm and damages in privacy torts, the PPA explicitly includes statutory damages provisions for infringement of privacy as per section 2 of the Act. Section 29A(b) provides that '(1) In a civil wrong-doing proceeding under section 4, the court may order that the defendant shall pay the plaintiff statutory damages that will not exceed 50,000 New Shekels. (2) In a proceeding under paragraph (1) in which it was proven that the infringement on privacy was made with intent to cause harm, the court may order that the defendant shall pay the plaintiff statutory damages that will not exceed double the amount in that paragraph.' These sums are linked to the general consumer price index and the basic sum as of January 2023 is approximately NIS 65,000.

404. These statutory damages do not apply to violations of the data protection provisions of the PPA. Moreover, statutory damages are available only to plaintiffs in individual claims, rather than in class actions due to the restriction on statutory damages in section 20(e) of the Class Action Act, 2006.

Chapter 5. Liability

§1. Introduction

405. The PPA and its peripheral regulations provide for three general types of liability that could be imposed on controllers, processors, database managers, security supervisors, or any person infringing privacy. These include criminal liability, civil liability, and administrative liability.

§2. Criminal Liability

406. Section 5 of the PPA, addressing privacy torts, provides that 'a person who wilfully infringes the privacy of another in any of the ways stated in sections 2(1), (3) to (7) and (9) to (11) is liable to imprisonment for a term of five years.'

407. As a general principle, substantiating criminal offences under Israeli law requires proving the *actus reus* of the offence and the *mens rea* of the offence in a general level of consciousness.[401] However, if a specific offence requires explicit intention, the *mens rea* for such offences includes the intention to cause the consequences of the offence.[402] The offence of section 5 of the PPA includes such intentional *mens rea* requirement and is thus reserved for act intended to infringe privacy at the criminal level.[403]

408. As opposed to section 5 of the PPA, section 31A of the Act provides for a list of strict liability offences applicable to whomever:

> (1) manages, possesses or uses a database in violation of the provisions of section 8; (2) provides incorrect particulars in an application for registration of a database as required in section 9; (3) fails to provide particulars or provides incorrect particulars in the notice accompanying a request to obtain information under section 11; (4) fails to comply with the provisions of sections 13 and 13A regarding the right to inspect information kept in a database or fails to correct information in accordance with the provisions of section 14; (5) enables access to a database in violation of the provisions of section 17A(a) or fails to provide to the Registrar documents or an affidavit in accordance with the provisions of section 17A(b); (6) fails to appoint a security supervisor in accordance with the provisions of section 17B; (7) manages or possesses a database used for direct mailing services, in violation of the provisions of sections 17D to 17F; (8) delivers information in violation of the provisions of sections 23B to 23E.

---

401. Penal Act, 1977, s. 20(a); *see also* Crim. A. 11/99 *Vinitzki v. State of Israel*, 53(2) PD 145 (1999).
402. Penal Act, 1977, s. 20(a)(1); *see also* LCrA 7153/99 *Elgad v. State of Israel*, 55(5) PD 729 (2001).
403. Crim. C. 2126/05 *Jarice v. State of Israel* (2006).

409. Thus, the strict liability offences of section 31A apply to many of the data protection provisions of the PPA, including database registration and purpose limitation, data subject rights, and data security. Given that these offences could be constituted without criminal intent or negligence, and may apply to conduct which is in the ordinary course of business, there is a relatively weaker penalty attached to such offences, of up to one year of imprisonment.[404] As of August 2022, we are unaware of indictments based solely on these offences.

410. Criminal proceedings and investigations under the PPA are generally initiated by the Database Registrar and the Attorney General, but the Database Registrar cannot issue indictments, a power that is reserved to the Attorney General.[405]

§3. Civil Liability

411. The PPA explicitly determines that a violation of both its privacy tort provisions and its data protection provisions constitute civil wrongs and thus affords a private cause of action. Accordingly, individuals whose privacy or data protection rights have been infringes can file civil claims and seek certain remedies as discussed in Chapter 4 above.

412. The main type of proceedings under the civil liability of the PPA is a private, individual or joint, civil claim. Such claims are filed with Magistrates or District courts depending on the amount of damages sought,[406] and, as discussed above, can yield statutory damages of up to NIS 50,000 (section 29A(b)(1)), and where the defendant acted maliciously, the sum can be doubled (section 29A(b)(2)). These sums are updated in line of the monthly index. As of January 2023, the sums are approximately NIS 65,000 for the ceiling of regular statutory damages and NIS 130,000 for malicious acts.

413. Another significant type of proceeding available for violations of the PPA is class action. The Class Action Act, 2006, allows plaintiffs to file motions to certify individual claims as class actions if certain conditions are met, and thus represent the entire class of plaintiffs with similar common causes of action.

414. The Class Action Act does not apply to any cause of action. Annex B of the Act sets forth a list of actionable types of causes of action that could be brought as class actions. While violations of the PPA are not, in and of themselves, actionable under Annex B, certain items in the Annex do allow framing privacy and data protection claims as class action.[407] For example, Annex B provides that claims brought by customers against businesses, as defined in the Consumer Protection

404. Note that s. 22 of the Penal Act, 1977 generally does not allow imprisonment under strict liability offences without *mens rea*.
405. *See* Chs 1–3 to this part.
406. *See* Courts Act [Consolidated Version], 1984, ss 40, 51.
407. CA 4110/18 *Doe v. Kadima Mada (Science Forward) Ltd.* (2019).

Act, 1981, against insurance companies, pension funds, banking corporations or financial services providers are actionable as class actions regardless of the cause of action sought.[408] Class actions are also available for causes of actions of employees against their employers in certain circumstances.[409] Yet, class actions against public bodies, such as municipalities, do not fit any of the items listed in Annex B, and in the absence of privacy from that list, are not actionable.[410]

415. While there is much criticism of the fact that Annex B does not explicitly allow class actions for any cause of action under the PPA, we note that, at least in consumer-related circumstances, courts have considered privacy and data protection causes of actions could be included in class actions, including where unpaid online services are concerned.[411]

416. The Class Action Act requires class plaintiffs to meet certain criteria for the cause of action to be certified as a class action, which may pose challenges in cases concerning privacy and data protection. First, plaintiffs must show that the cause of action shows a factual or legal question that is common to the entire class members. Second, they must show that a class action is the most efficient and beneficial way to conduct the proceedings for the benefit of the class members.[412] Third, they must show that the matters of all class members will be managed appropriately.[413] Fourth, they must show that the matters of all class members are managed in good faith.[414] In addition, class actions proceedings do not acknowledge statutory damages, and thus actual damages, including non-pecuniary damages should be proved.

417. These requirements may, at times, pose challenges to privacy and data protection-related cases, especially with respect to the communality requirement that may be difficult to establish when different types of data subjects, types of data, or types of processing were conducted with respect to each of the class members, as well as with respect to the types of harms caused to each such member. Some courts have raised questions regarding the suitability of class actions in certain circumstances of violations of privacy and data protection rights due to the lack of communality of the type of harm caused to the class members.[415]

§4. Administrative Liability

418. The PPA provides a framework for regulatory enforcement of its data protection provisions. As discussed in Chapters 1–3 above, it constituted the Database

408. Class Action Act, 2006, Annex B, items 1-3A.
409. *Ibid*, Annex B, item 10(1).
410. *See, e.g.*, CA 4110/18 *Doe v. Kadima Mada (Science Forward) Ltd.* (2019).
411. MCP (Tel Aviv, District) 23305/06 *Rothschild v. Partner Communications Ltd.* (2009), para. 18; Class A. (Tel Aviv, District) 26737-09-15 *Yahoo Inc. v. Lenual* (2017); *Doe v. Kadima.*
412. Class Action Act, 2006, s. 8(a)(2).
413. *Ibid.*, s. 8(a)(3).
414. *Ibid*, s. 8(a)(4).
415. Class. A. (Be'er Sheva, District) 41837-09-16 *Doe v. Daka90 Ltd.* (2019); CA 4110/18 *Doe v. Kadima Mada (Science Forward) Ltd.* (2019), para. 9; Class A. 7322-10-18 (Tel Aviv, District) *Axelrod v. Facebook Inc.* (2022), p. 111.

Registrar (and, in turn, the PP Authority), which has both criminal and administrative investigations and enforcement powers.

419. The Database Registrar may impose certain sanctions.[416] As a matter of practice, the Database Registrar initiates administrative inspections and investigations regularly, either for reviewing a sample of organizations in a specific sector, due to data breach notifications or due to complaints issued with the Registrar.[417]

§5. Defences and Exemptions

420. The PPA provides for three categories of exemptions and defences from civil and criminal liability under the Act – general and specific exemptions, good faith conduct defences for privacy infringements and a general *de minimis* defence.

421. Section 18 of the PPA provides a list of defences for infringement of privacy under sections 4 and 5 of the Act related to traditional privacy torts, reads as follows:

(1) The infringement was committed by way of a publication protected under section 13 of the Defamation (Protection) Law, 5725 – 1965;
(2) The defendant or accused committed the infringement in good faith and in any of the following circumstances:
   (a) He did not know and need not have known that an infringement of privacy might occur; (b) the infringement was committed in circumstances in which the infringer was under a legal, moral, social or professional obligation to commit it;
   (c) The infringement was committed in defence of a legitimate personal interest of the infringer;
   (d) The infringement was committed in the lawful pursuit of the infringer's occupation and in the ordinary course of his work, so long as it was not committed by way of publication;
   (e) The infringement was committed by way of taking a photograph, or of publishing a photograph taken, in the public domain, and the injured party appears in it accidentally;
   (f) The infringement was committed by way of a publication protected under paragraphs (4) to (11) of section 15 of the PDA 1965;
(3) The infringement involved a public interest justifying it in the circumstances of the case, provided that, if the infringement was committed by way of publication, the publication was not untruthful.

416. Further elaborated in Ch. 6 below.
417. Privacy Protection Authority, Annual Report for the Year 2021, at 18–32 (2022).

422. These defences do not apply to data protection violations under Part B of the PPA. Note that the defences of sub-sections 18(1), and 18(2)(f) reference the PDA 1965, and mainly relate to circumstance pertaining to freedom of speech and public interest.

423. As for the defences in sub-section (2), these are restricted to actions conducted in good faith by the alleged infringer; courts have ruled that such good faith should be examined from a subjective perspective.[418] Section 20 of the PPA provides a set of presumptions as to the good faith of an alleged infringer raising a defence claim as follows:

(a) Where the accused or defendant proves that he committed infringement of privacy under any of the circumstances referred to in section 18(2) and that it did not exceed the limits reasonable under those circumstances, he shall be presumed to have committed it in good faith.
(b) The accused or defendant shall be presumed not to have committed the infringement of privacy in good faith if in committing it he knowingly went further than was reasonably necessary for the purposes of the matters protected by section 18(2).
(c) An accused person or defendant who sets up the plea provided by section 18(2)(b) or (d) shall be presumed not to have infringed privacy in good faith if he infringed it in violation of the rules or principles of professional ethics applying to him by law or accepted by members of the profession to which he belongs; however, this presumption will not apply if the infringement was caused in circumstances that the accused person or defendant acted according to a legal duty that was imposed on him.

424. Courts have ruled that the section 18 defences do not form a general permission to infringe privacy in the outlined circumstances, rather only function as after-the-fact defences. Thus, organizations wilfully initiating privacy infringing conduct based on such defences, cannot enjoy them.[419] Thus, it appears that the various defences under section 18(2) – acting without knowing of the infringement, infringing privacy due to a legal, moral or social obligation, defending a personal interest of the infringer or conducting the infringement in the lawful ordinary course of business, all require some sense of necessity and acting in a manner that is not otherwise unlawful.

425. Courts have mainly reviewed such defences in the context of private investigations conducted by certified private investigators who infringed the privacy of their investigation subjects for the benefit of the investigation. While courts were generally reluctant to grant the defences set forth in section 18(2)(b) and (c),[420] they

418. Crim. A. 5026/97 *Gal'am v. State of Israel* (1999).
419. HCJ 6650/04 *Doe v. Regional Rabbinical Court, Netanya*, 61(1) PD 581, 10-607(2006).
420. CC (Hadera, Magistrate) 2293/08 *Abu Shakra Ltd. v. Yanir Communications Ltd.*, paras 15–17 (2011); CC (Jerusalem, District) 9562/07 *Darshan v. Menorah Insurance Company Ltd.*, (2012), paras 13–16.

were keen, in certain circumstances, to provide the defence under section 18(2)(d) provided that such private investigators did not otherwise violate any professional ethics or laws in conducting their investigations.[421]

426. In addition, section 19 of the PPA provides two general exemptions from liability under any provision of the Act. Section 19(a) provides that 'No person shall bear responsibility under this Law for an act which he is empowered to do by law.' This exemption is generally available for governmental entities and public bodies operating under explicit authorization by law,[422] but may conceivably apply to private organizations when processing personal data pursuant to a mandatory legal requirement such as in the context of providing mandatory labour-related benefits, reporting under anti-money-laundering legislation, or retaining tax and accounting related data.[423]

427. Section 19(b) provides that 'a security authority or a person employed by it or acting on its behalf shall bear no responsibility under this Law for an infringement reasonably committed within the scope of their functions and for the purpose of carrying them out.'

428. The exemption under section 19(b) does not provide an independent authorization for law enforcement and security agencies to process personal data, rather it acknowledges any external explicit authorization to do so in other laws.[424] Courts explained that the exemption is subject to reasonableness and proportionality tests such that not any infringing action of a security agency is exempt from liability.[425]

429. Lastly, section 6 of the PPA provides that 'no right to bring a civil or criminal action under this Law shall accrue through an infringement of no real significance'. This is a *de minimis* defence explicitly acknowledged by the PPA. Courts have granted such defences in relatively rare circumstances of actual insignificance and no apparent harm. One court has recently acknowledged such defence in a class action alleging violation of the data security duties under the PPA, explaining that given that no harm was allegedly proved, section 6 applies.[426]

421. Crim. A. 5026/97 *Gal'am v. State of Israel* (1999); Crim. C. (Nazareth, Magistrate) 3159/05 *State of Israel v. Rosenthal* (2008).
422. HCJ 4455/19 *Tebeka Advocacy for Equality & Justice for Ethiopian Israelis v. Israel Police* (2021), para. 32.
423. Bank. C. (Tel Aviv, District) 32225-02-12 *Nissanov v. Nissanov* (2016).
424. *See* Part III, Ch. 1 above.
425. *Tebeka*, at para. 32; HCJ 3809/08 *Association for Civil Rights in Israel v. Israel Police* (2012).
426. Class A. (Tel Aviv, District) 7322-10-18 *Axelrod v. Facebook Inc.* (2022).

Chapter 6. Penalties

430. The PPA includes two general types of offences:[427] One is the wilful infringement of privacy, and the other is the statutory strict liability data protection offence. In addition, the Administrative Offences Regulations (Administrative Fine – Protection of Privacy), 2004 provide for a limited set of administrative fines for specific data protection violations of the PPA.

431. The wilful infringement of privacy offence entails a maximum penalty of five years of imprisonment. There is no minimum mandatory penalty, and thus courts have discretion over the actual penalty imposed which could range from criminal fines instead of imprisonment of up to NIS 226,000, to actual imprisonment.[428]

432. The strict liability offences under the PPA, which pertain to violations of its data protection provisions, provide for a penalty of up to one year of imprisonment. This effectively means that save for extreme circumstances, penalties will be limited to service hours or criminal fines of up to NIS 29,200.

433. The administrative fines under the Administrative Offences Regulations vary between its different provisions, but range between up to NIS 5,000 for individuals and NIS 25,000 for incorporated entities.

434. The Database Registrar is authorized to impose another significant sanction as part of its administrative investigation capacities. Section 10(f) of the PPA provides that 'Where the possessor or owner of a database infringes any provision of this Law or the regulations thereunder, or fails to comply with a request made to him by the Registrar, the Registrar may suspend the registration for a period that he shall determine or cancel the registration of the database in the Register, provided that prior to the suspension or cancellation the owner of the database was given the opportunity to be heard.'[429]

435. This effectively means that the Database Registrar has the power to order organizations to cease using their databases, either temporarily or permanently, which is a relatively severe sanction, especially in data-driven organizations.

---

427. *See also* Ch. 5 above.
428. Penal Act, 1977, s. 61(a)(4).
429. Database Registrar, Annual Report for the Year 2016, at 24–25 (2022).

Part IX. Specific Processing Situations

Chapter 1. Processing for Journalistic Purposes and Academic, Artistic or Literary Expression

§1. Introduction

436. The PPA's regulation of databases does not contain any direct references to processing of personal data for journalistic purposes, academic, artistic, or literary expression. Other parts of the PPA, regulating privacy torts, contain some relevant principles and rules in this regard. Some additional laws may apply in specific contexts, e.g., health research.

437. When public bodies are involved in such processing, the constitutional dimension of privacy may come into play.[430]

438. To the extent that other laws or legal principles pertaining to the above kinds of processing conflict with the PPA, courts are likely to engage in balancing, within the legislative parameters.

§2. Journalistic Purposes

439. Freedom of expression and freedom of the press are not enumerated in the Basic Laws. Nevertheless, the Supreme Court has repeatedly acknowledged these rights, and have protected them in various contexts.[431] Often, free speech rights and free press interests were balanced with other interests, such as national security or public order.

440. Absent legislative references to processing personal data for journalist purposes, courts treat such processing like other kinds of processing. When a news

430. *See* Part I, Ch. 1.
431. For free speech in Israeli law, *see* HCJ 243/62 *Film Studios in Israel Ltd. v. Levy*, 16 PD 2408 (1962); HCJ 2557/05 *Mate-Harov v. Israel Police* 62(1) PD 200 (2006). For freedom of the press in Israeli law, *see* MP 298/86 *Zitrin v. The Disciplinary Court of the Tel Aviv District Bar Association*, 41(2) PD 337, 360–361 (1987); ACH 2121/12 *Doe v. Dayan-Orbach*, 67(1) PD 667 (2014).

website curated a webpage dedicated to legal proceedings of a British–Israeli businessperson, the district court concluded that the webpage was a 'database' under the PPA's definitions (section 7), that some of the contents were publicly available, namely judicial decisions and hence exempt from registration (per section 8(d)), but also that some were not publicly available, namely various litigation documents. Accordingly, the court ruled that the non-public material should have been registered with the Database Registrar, and without such registration, holding it was unlawful, and the webpage should be removed.[432] Defendant's arguments about freedom of expression were mentioned, but did not affect the decision.

441. If plaintiff frames their arguments not as a matter of data protection but of traditional privacy torts, journalistic purposes may come into play, by way of defences, under the PPA's Chapter C.[433] The defences are available for both privacy torts and criminal charges (section 18). There are three groups of defences available. The first includes defences for certain publications made by public officials in their official role (section 18(1)); the second refers to several situations, subject to a preliminary condition of acting in good faith (section 18(2)); the third group is a public interest defence. We elaborate on these.

442. First, the PPA, section 18(1) incorporates defences under section 13 in the PDA 1965. This section refers to publication in official contexts: A publication by a Knesset member for which the member is immune (section 13(1)); a report in a cabinet meeting (section 13(2)), publication by the government or on its behalf (section 13(3)); a publication by the state comptroller (section 12(4)); a publication by a judge in the context of a hearing or in an opinion (section 13(5)); and a publication by a member of an official inquiry committee (section 13(6)).[434] Other situations are relevant to journalists – referring to the manner in which they report about the previous six situations. A correct and fair report about judicial comments and by members of inquiry committee – do not give rise to a tort or an offence (section 13(7));[435] the same, regarding a publication in a public session of an international court, or the Jewish Agency (section 13(8)); a publication that was required by law or an order of an authorized agency (section 13(9)); a correct and fair report of public registries (section 13(10)), and a correct and fair report about the previous situations, other than cabinet meetings (section 13(11)).[436]

432. OM (Tel Aviv, District) 9333-12-19 *Soriano v. The Seventh Eye* (2022).

433. *See* Part VIII, Ch. 6.

434. *See, e.g.*, CA (Tel Aviv, District) 43991-03-14 *HaEfrati v. Jackont* (2015).

435. In a dissenting opinion, Justice Elyakim Rubinstein found that a journalist report exceeded reporting criminal charges, and was incorrect, hence, in his view, the defence should have failed. *See* ACH 2121/13 *Doe v. Dayan-Orbach*, 67(1) PD 667, 811 (2014).

436. For these defences in defamation law, *see, e.g.*, T. Gidron, *Defamation Law in Turbulence: Does Israel Need 'Libel Reform'*?, 46(1) Isr. L. Rev. 95, 109–111 (2013); K. Ghanayim, M. Kremnitzer & B. Shnoor, *Libel Law de lege lata and lege ferenda* 359–382 (Sacher & Nevo 2d ed. 2019) [Hebrew].

443. Second, section 18(2) lists six situations that are all subject to a preliminary condition of acting in good faith. The situations are:

(a) That the defendant did not know or could not know about the possibility of violating privacy. This defence would be less relevant to journalistic work, as journalists are expected to be aware of privacy as both a legal right and an ethical norm.
(b) When the infringer was under a legal, moral, social or professional obligation to commit it.[437] This defence may be more relevant to journalists.[438]
(c) When infringement was committed in defence of a legitimate personal interest of the infringer. This defence may fit people in social interactions, and are less relevant in the journalistic context.
(d) When 'the infringement was committed in the lawful pursuit of the infringer's occupation and in the ordinary course of his work, so long as it was not committed by way of publication.' – while journalists may claim that they were doing their job, this defence may be available only in actions regarding the collection of data, but not for its publication, for which the journalists would have to seek alternative defences.
(e) When 'the infringement was committed by way of taking a photograph, or of publishing a photograph taken, in the public domain, and the injured party appears in it accidently.' This situation is indeed relevant to journalists, if the conditions set here are met.
(f) The last situation again refers to the PDA, this time referring to sections 15(4)–15(11) thereof. These situations refer to expressing one's opinion on a public figure's official actions; on a party to litigation in public hearings; critique of literary, scientific or artistic that was published; and similar activities.[439]

444. The Supreme Court clarified that good faith is subjective, namely, that the person who violated another's privacy believed that he is permitted to act in that manner, under the defence.[440]

445. The PPA provides guidance as to the meaning of good faith under this group of cases. Section 20(a) sets a presumption of good faith when the harm was reasonable in the specific circumstance, and section 20(b) creates a presumption of lack of good faith when defendant knowingly harmed plaintiff more than needed to achieve the purposes listed in section 18(2), namely the six situations mentioned above.

---

437. When private investigator entered private homes under pretext and took intimate photos, meant to serve as evidence in divorce proceedings, the Supreme Court rejected their argument that they were under a professional duty to do so. *See* Crim. A. 5026/97 *Gal'am v. State of Israel* (1999).
438. *See, e.g.*, CC (Tel Aviv, District) 40124-02-14 *Ofek v. Channel Israel 10 – New Broadcasting Channel Ltd.* (2022), para. 132. The court, in dismissing a defamation case, found that defendant journalist acted in good faith, both under the PDA and under s. 18(2)(b) of the PPA.
439. *See, e.g.*, LCA 10520/03 *Ben-Gvir v. Dankner* (2006).
440. *See* HCJ 6650/04 *Doe v. Regional Rabbinical Court, Netanya*, 61(1) PD 581, 609 (2006).

446. Another way to unpack good faith is found in norms of professional ethics: Section 20(c) sets a presumption of lack of good faith if defendant's actions breached the ethical norms. This presumption refers to the defences listed in section 18(2)(b) – acting under a legal, moral, social, or professional obligation, and in section 18(2)(d) – an action done during a lawful pursuit of the infringer's occupation. Journalist ethics typically contain the protection of privacy, albeit in broad terms.[441]

447. Third, section 18(3) contains a general, public interest defence, which is not conditioned on good faith: 'The infringement involved a public interest justifying it in the circumstances of the case, provided that, if the infringement was committed by way of publication, the publication was not untruthful.' Courts clarified that the public interest does not mean what interests the public, but a public interest per se.[442]

§3. Academic Purposes

448. Similarly, the PPA does not contain any direct reference to academic processing – neither teaching nor research. Thus, regular rules about data protection apply.[443] In specific cases, such as medical or genetic research, additional, specific rules apply. If the processing of data for research purposes is also a violation of traditional privacy torts, then the defences listed in section 18 and discussed in the previous paragraphs, may be applicable. Note that these defences focus mostly on publication, rather than the collection or processing of the data.

449. When the academic research conducted contains health data, the Patients' Rights Act, 1996 should be consulted, in addition to the PPA. The Patients' Rights Act contains a general duty of confidentiality regarding medical data (section 19), but it allows transferring medical data to other parties in some cases, two of which are relevant for academic processing. First, medical data can be transferred to

441. The Professional Ethics Code of the Israeli Press Council (which is a private association), lists privacy as an ethical principle (s. 10), *see* http://www.moaza.co.il/BRPortal/br/P102.jsp?arc=26627&printable=full [Hebrew]. Section 10(2) states: 'Journalists shall not publish anything which may harm a person's privacy, without his consent, unless there is a public interest and in an appropriate manner.' This section echoes the PPA's defence set in s. 18(3), discussed in the following paragraph. The result may be that the legislative separation between defences that require good faith and those that do not, is blurred. A court, when examining a defence under s. 18 of the PPA that sets a prerequisite of good faith, will apply the presumption set in s. 20, which will lead the court to the ethical code, which will insert the public interest, an independent defence that does not require good faith as a prerequisite. For applying s. 20(c) and turning to the ethics code, *see, e.g.*, CC (Herzliya, Magistrate) *Doe v. Semel* (2016), paras 70–72.

442. *See, e.g.*, CA 439/88 *Database Registrar v. Ventura*, 48(3) PD 808, 827 (1994); Crim. A. 11793/05 *Israeli News Co. Ltd. v. State of Israel* (2006), at para. 38; Z. Segal, *The Right to Privacy*, 9 TAU L. Rev. 175, 198 (1983) [Hebrew].

443. Higher education institutions enjoy academic freedom, including regarding research, *see* Council for Higher Education Act, 1958, s. 15. However, this freedom is constrained by various laws and regulations regarding research in human subjects, as well as the PPA, regarding data subjects, as explained in this chapter. *See, e.g.*, A. Carmi, *supra* n. 109, 1306.

another party with the patient's consent (section 20(a)(1)), and second, it is permitted to hand over medical data for the purpose of publication in a scientific journal, or for purposes of research or teaching according to the Minister of Health's instructions, as long as identifying data is not revealed (section 20(a)(7), and section 32(4)). As of December 2022, no such instructions were issued.

450. Medical research conducted in hospitals is subject to an additional legal regime, of the Helsinki Ethical Principles for Medical Research Involving Human Subjects, which were integrated in Israeli law by way of regulations in 1980.[444]

451. Research of genetic data is subject to specific rules, under the GDA.[445] Such research is permitted only if the study was approved (section 3(c) of the GDA). Informed consent for DNA sampling for research should be in writing (section 11(b)). The GDA waives the consent requirement (under section 11) and the duty to notify the subject (under section 12) when the genetic data is used for research, that earned approval, which is based only on unidentified DNA samples, or de-identified samples, if re-identification is impossible 'in any manner' (section 13). Retention of genetic data is permitted, if identifying data was removed, unless the subject has consented in writing to the retention of identified samples (section 15(b)(2)). The General Director of the Ministry of Health is authorized to issue rules as to such retention (section 15(c)). Similarly, the holder of genetic data may transfer it to another party, for teaching, research or publication in a scientific journal, if the research was approved, and if the data were transferred without identifying information or that the participant has consented, in writing, to such transfer, prior to the transfer (section 23). There are further rules regarding minors (sections 24(4), 26(a), 26(b)). Security bodies may use DNA samples that they possess for research related to forensic identification, intelligence gathering for national security purposes, and identification of bodies (section 32(a)(4)), or, for any other purpose – with the written consent of the person (section 32(a)(5)).

452. Research of umbilical cord blood is regulated in the Umbilical Cord Blood (Public Repository) Regulations, 2012.[446] A party who may consent to the collection and retention of the blood in the first place, may provide consent for using the blood for research, but if the sample cannot be frozen and stored, and if the research was approved (section 18).

§4. Artistic or Literary Purposes

453. The PPA does not contain any direct reference to processing of personal data for artistic or literary purposes. However, as with processing of data for

444. People's Health Regulations (Medical Research Involving Human Subjects), 1980. Carmi, *supra* n. 109, at 1314.
445. For background and discussion, *see* Part I, Ch. 4, and discussion in Carmi, *supra* n. 109, at 1397–1408.
446. T. Trigger, *The Regulation of Fertility Services in Israel*, in *Regulating Regulation: Law and Policy* 269 (Y. Blank, D. Levi-Faur & R. Kreitner eds, Tel Aviv U. Press 2016) [Hebrew].

journalistic purposes, the PPA's Chapters A and C may apply, dealing with privacy torts and defences.

454. When an author published a romantic book, supposedly fictional, but one that revealed intimate data about his former partner, the Supreme Court juxtaposed the woman's privacy with the author's right to freedom of expression, which includes artistic and literary forms of expression.[447] The Court emphasized the importance of both rights, that the legislature has determined their balance in the PPA, but that the PPA should be interpreted in light of the Basic Law.[448] The Court considered the importance of the rights, the likelihood of violating them, and the extent of the harm.[449] The Court then articulated the balancing guideline: When the harm to privacy is in its external parameters and the harm to free speech is at its core, free speech should prevail, and vice versa.[450] Applying this test to the circumstances resulted in confirming a permanent restraining order, prohibiting the publication of the book.

447. CA 8954/11 *Doe v. Roe*, 66(3) PD 691 (2014).
448. *Ibid.*, at para. 68.
449. *Ibid.*, at para. 122.
450. *Ibid.*, at paras 126 and 136.

Chapter 2. Processing of Personal Information Versus Public Access to Official Documents

§1. Introduction

455. The interface between data protection law and the public's access to official documents is not straightforward. The main legal intersections are of privacy (and data protection) and freedom of information, access to archives, and access to judicial cases. The availability of official documents is part of the broader principle of transparency, which Israeli law has been promoting at least since the late 1990s. Transparency is not absolute, and is limited when it is in conflict with rights or other public interests.

456. In a previous chapter,[451] we discussed a data subject's right to access personal data about them, which is held by another. In the current chapter, we discuss access to official documents that contain data about *other* data subjects.

§2. Data Protection and Freedom of Information

457. The right to access official documents is associated in Israeli law with the right to freedom of expression (which is not explicitly enumerated in the Basic Law, but has been recognized as a constitutional right).[452] The right is anchored and regulated in the Freedom of Information Act, 1998 (FOIA). The Supreme Court instructed that the balance between privacy and freedom of information is 'horizontal', between two equal rights.[453]

458. Chapter D of the PPA forbids public bodies to transfer data to private entities (section 23B), with some exceptions (section 23C), but none are related to access to official documents. This limitation could have shut the door on FOIA, but section 35 clarifies that the PPA does not derogate from the provisions of any other law. The Supreme Court avoided the issue for some time, but eventually clarified that the PPA sets a general legal regime, whereas FOIA is a concrete and later legal regime.[454]

459. FOIA's section 1 states: 'Every Israeli citizen or resident has the right to receive information from a public authority, according to this Act.' Section 9 lists

451. Part IV, Ch. 2.

452. *See, e.g.*, AA 398/07 *The Freedom of Information Movement v. Tax Authority*, 63(1) PD 284, 377 (2008), and in the literature, *see, e.g.*, Y. Rabin & R. Peled, *The Constitutional Right to Receive Information*, in *The Dorner Book* 463 (S. Almog, D. Beinisch & Y. Rotem eds, Nevo 2009) [Hebrew].

453. *See Tax Authority*, *ibid.*, at 336. *See also* A. Barak, *Freedom of Information and the Court*, 3 Kiryat HaMishpat 95 (2003) [Hebrew]. For criticism of this framing, *see* M. Birnhack, *Free Information, Private Data*, in *Transparency and Corruption* 183 (N. Arad ed., Nevo 2021) [Hebrew].

454. AA 7678/16 *Drucker v. Freedom of Information Supervisor, Prime Minister's Office*, para. 17 (2017).

various exceptions, one of which relates to privacy: Section 9(a) instructs that a public authority shall not hand over information which is one of these ... '(3) Information that its disclosure consists a violation of privacy according to the PPA, unless the disclosure is permitted by law.' Public authorities occasionally rely on this exception, arguing that due to their duty to protect data subjects' privacy, they cannot disclose the data in freedom of information procedures. For example, the Tax Authority refused to disclose names of people who paid large fines instead of being charged ('Get out of jail card');[455] the Government Companies Authority refused to disclose names of candidates to the position of directors in government companies, and were disqualified, citing privacy concerns in both cases.[456]

460. FOIA's reference to the PPA leaves open various questions. For example, the PPA may acknowledge that a privacy violation took place, but nevertheless, that the defendant or the accused are not liable, due to one of the PPA's defences. It is unclear how FOIA should treat such a situation.[457]

461. This legislative bundle left courts somewhat confused.[458] However, FOIA provides a convenient way out of the legislative complexity. Section 17(d) empowers the court to order the disclosure of the information at stake, either in whole or in part, if it finds that the public interest in disclosure exceeds the benefits of non-disclosure. This authorization is not a guideline for judicial review of the public authority's refusal to disclose data, but rather, an independent power for the judges to assess for themselves the benefits and costs of such disclosure. This is an unusual judicial power.[459] Courts have applied this power to resolve various privacy/FOIA conflicts, including the option of setting various conditions. In one case, a tax-consulting firm asked a municipality to hand over data about property in its jurisdiction, including a list of residents' holdings. The municipality refused. The Supreme Court ordered the disclosure of data about property without identifying information, and ordered the municipality to enable residents interested to opt-in, and consent to transfer of their data.[460]

§3. Access to Archival Material

462. The Archives Act, 1955 regulates the preservation of archival material, defined there as any material held by a state organ. Section 10(a) of this Act states that 'Every person may review archival material deposited in the State Archive, but this right may be limited by regulations.' Such regulations were issued, and they

455. *Tax Authority*.
456. AA 9341/05 *The Freedom of Information Movement v. Government Companies Authority* (2009).
457. For discussion, *see* Birnhack, *supra* n. 450, at 190–191.
458. *See, e.g.*, comments to this effect: AA 7744/10 *National Insurance of Israel v. Mangal*, 66(1) PD 112, para. 15 (2012); *Government Companies Authority*. *See also* Y. Arbel & T. Schwartz Altshuler, *Information Wants to Be Free: Implementing the Freedom of Information Act in Israel* 165, 170 (Israel Democracy Institute 2008) [Hebrew].
459. For the rarity of the power, *see Drucker*, at para. 23.
460. AA 1386/07 *Municipality of Hadera v. Shenrom Ltd.* (2012).

contain limiting access for the purpose of protecting privacy of people who may be mentioned therein, for seventy years.[461] The regulations refer to the PPA. The seventy-year period may be shortened in some cases. The regulations extend this protection also to deceased people.[462]

463. The Supreme Court addressed some cases in which access was limited for national security reasons,[463] but no cases regarding privacy were found.

§4. Access to Judicial Records

464. The Basic Law: The Judiciary sets the principle of open courts as a constitutional norm. The Courts Act [Consolidated Version], 1984 further elaborates on open courts (section 68(a)), and permits a judge to hold a hearing behind closed doors in some cases (section 68(b)), such as national security, or to protect a minor, a person with cognitive or mental disability, a victim of sexual violation, and similar situations. The Act prohibits the publication of a hearing that was conducted behind closed doors (section 70(a)), and affords the judge with discretion to prohibit any publication about a court hearing, in order to protect the safety of a party to the litigation, or 'to prevent substantial harm to privacy.'[464]

465. The result is a series of default rules determining whether in a specific situation, the court doors are open as a default – but, nevertheless, a judge may determine otherwise, or the opposite default rule, that the doors are closed, but, nevertheless, a judge may permit publications about the trial and hearings.[465]

466. Special regulations determine that the list of cases to be tried should be open and accessible, as well as the judicial decisions which the law does not bar from publication.[466] The actual court files are open to the parties to the litigation;[467] any other non-party may petition the court that adjudicates the case to allow such access.[468] The court may set conditions for such access, including omitting details and undertaking other measures to prevent identification of parties.[469] The head of the Courts' Administration may issue a general access permit, if there is a public interest.[470] This option facilitates journalists' access.

461. *See* Archives Regulation (Access to Archival Material Deposited in the State Archive), 2010, s. 8(b)(2).
462. Archives Regulation, s. 8(c)(2).
463. HCJ 15/19 *Hazkani v. Head of the Israel Security Service* (2021); HCJ 3345/19 *Kaplan v. State Archive* (2021).
464. *See, e.g.*, LCA 3788/06 *Yefet v. Yedioth Ahronoth Ltd.* (2012).
465. *See, e.g.*, LCA 3007/02 *Itzhak v. Mozes*, 56(6) PD 592 (2002).
466. Courts and Labour Court Regulations (Access to Files), 2003, s. 2; Crim. C. (Tel Aviv, District) 66313-12-15 *Meuhedet Health Insurance v. Eliash* (2018).
467. Courts and Labour Court Regulations, s. 3; Crim. A. 5031/94 *Ben-Natan v. State of Israel* (2013).
468. Courts and Labour Court Regulations, ss 4(a), 4(b); HCJ 5917/97 *ACRI v. Ministry of Justice* (2009); LCA 1675/21 *Doe v. State of Israel* (2021).
469. Courts and Labour Court Regulations, s. 4(f).
470. *Ibid.*, s. 5.

Chapter 3. Processing of the National Identification Number

467. All residents in Israel must be registered with the national population registry. At first registration (e.g., at birth, or when becoming a citizen), each resident is designated a national identification number.[471] Residents, for this purpose, include citizens, immigrants, and those who hold a permanent residency permit.[472] The national identification number is included in the official identification card (in Hebrew: *Teudat Zehut*, literally meaning identity card, rather than identification):

468. The ID number plays a crucial role in daily lives of Israeli residents. As the Supreme Court commented:

> There is a connection between the use of a person's identity number and his right to privacy. Indeed, the identity number is not merely a stream of digits. The number, which is given to a resident of Israel at birth, accompanies him in all his steps. It appears in the identity card, in the passport, driving license, bank documents, military documents, tax registrations, various legal documents, transactions he is party to, and, after death – in a death certificate and inheritance orders. The identity number cannot be changed and it is not erased when the taxpayer dies or leaves the country. Thus, the number can indicate information and data about a person's actions, businesses, the style, and characteristics of its holder in diverse fields, until there is a unity between the person and the identity number.[473]

469. Accordingly, the Court concluded that the transfer of the ID number from police officers to tax collectors in that case, the processing of the data and making decisions based on it, violated privacy.[474] In another case, the Court ruled that while a police officer may ask a person to present their identification card even if they are not suspect, absent such suspicion the officers are prohibited from using the data included in the card to perform additional police inquiries.[475]

470. Following data breaches and leaks, large portions of the national population registry were made available online, including names and identification numbers.[476] The Database Registrar issued an instruction, clarifying that authenticating users based solely on data included in the leaked registry, is insufficient to meet the data security requirement, under section 17 of the PPA.[477] In other words: Service

471. Population Registry Act, 1965, s. 2(b).
472. *Ibid.*, s. 1(a).
473. HCJ 6824/07 *Manna v. Tax Authority*, 64(2) PD 479, 517–518 (2010).
474. *Ibid.*, citing M. Birnhack, *Consent and Control: The Theoretical Basis of the Right to Privacy*, 11 Law & Gov. Israel 11, 42 (2008) [Hebrew].
475. HCJ 4455/19 *Tebeka Advocacy for Equality & Justice for Ethiopian Israelis v. Israel Police* (2021).
476. Those responsible for the leak were charged and sentenced. *See* Crim. C. (Tel Aviv, Magistrate) 24441-05-12 *State of Israel v. Bilik* (2016).
477. Database Registrar, Instruction 1-2010 Minimum Requirements for identity Authentication of Data Subjects for the Purpose of Access to Data about him, Held in a Database (2010).

providers who wish to enable users access to their account, cannot rely only on identification number, as there is a concern that others might impersonate as the user.

471. In the context of privacy torts, the Supreme Court found that the identification number is considered 'information on a person's private affairs', under section 2(9) of the PPA, which sets the purpose limitation principle. Accordingly, the Court found that a private database including names and ID numbers of people who failed to repay debts, where the data was collected from cheques without consent, constituted a privacy tort.[478]

478. CA 439/88 *Database Registrar v. Ventura*, 48(3) PD 808 (1994).

Chapter 4. Processing in the Context of Employment

§1. Introduction

472. The PPA does not treat employment-related personal data processing differently than any other processing of personal data. Employment-related personal data are not directly considered sensitive data (although the employer may have data about the economic situation of the employee). The DataSec Regulations generally consider databases that contain data on employees as low security level ones (except when public bodies are concerned).[479]

473. However, Labour Courts, in a line of judicial decisions, created a de facto separate framework for the processing of personal data of employees, at least in the sense of legal bases for processing, proportionality requirements, and restrictions on certain types of processing in sensitive circumstances.

§2. Legal Basis for Processing, Proportionality and Transparency

474. In several cases, the National Labour Court, the highest instance adjudicating labour-related disputes,[480] explained that although consent is the sole legal basis for processing under the PPA, consent is inherently suspicious in employment relationships due to the imbalance of powers between employers and employees. Thus, the Court deemed consent alone to be insufficient to establish a lawful ground for the processing of employee data.[481]

475. The Court added several factors to be considered when the lawful processing by an employer is contested. The Court explained that while informed consent is a prerequisite to lawful processing by employers, the following factors should be considered as well:

476. First, the employer must adopt a clear policy on the processing of personal data of employees, covering all aspects of the envisaged processing.[482] This requirement is coupled with a transparency obligation, in which such policy should be communicated to the employees, and, if a labour union exists, the policy should be drafted in consultation with the union.[483]

479. DataSec Regulations, Annex I, item 1(2).
480. The Supreme Court, acting as the HCJ, may decide to hear petitions against the National Labour Court's decisions.
481. LA (National) 90/08 *Issakov-Inbar v. State of Israel – The Commissioner for the Women's Labour Law* (2011); LA (National) 7541-04-14 *New Histadrut (General Organization of Workers in Israel) v. Qalansawe Municipality* (2017); T. Golan, *The Examining and the Observing Eye: Regulation and Policing of Employee Behavior in the Workplace*, in *Regulating Regulation: Law and Policy* 515 (Y. Blank, D. Levi-Faur & R. Kreitner eds, Tel Aviv U. Press 2016) [Hebrew].
482. *Qalansawe*, at para. 111(a).
483. *Ibid.*, at paras 111(b)–(c).

477. Second, the processing activities should be proportionate to the envisaged purpose of processing and the legitimate interest of the employer. This means that alternative processing measures should be considered, to assess whether their utility is sufficient and they are less harmful to the employees' privacy.[484] In this context, the Court will also review the sanctions, if any, that employers impose on employees who refuse to certain processing activities, in terms of proportionality and legitimacy.[485]

478. The above principles were adopted by the Court in circumstances involving monitoring email communications and processing biometric data as an attendance mechanism.

§3. CCTV CAMERAS IN WORKPLACES

479. The PPA does not explicitly refer to CCTVs in any context, let alone in the workplace context.

480. The PP Authority issued guidelines on the use of CCTV cameras in workplaces.[486] Applying the legitimacy, proportionality, and transparency requirements set forth by the National Labour Court from the context of email monitoring, the Authority provided several limitations on the use of CCTV cameras in employment contexts.

481. First, the Authority reiterated that the cameras should only be installed for legitimate purposes and any data retained must only be processed for such specific purposes, as shall be set forth in a written policy communication to employees.[487]

482. Second, the Authority explained that cameras should never be hidden to employees and that the location of the cameras should be communicated to all employees covered by such cameras.[488]

483. Third, the Authority generally prohibited installing cameras that cover private areas in the workplace such as individual workstations, restrooms, dining rooms, etc. This rule may have exceptions in particular cases such as employees working remotely in a small space with a safe or cashier.[489]

484. Fourth, the Authority required employees to set a proportionate retention period for the footage of such cameras, in light of the legitimate purpose established by the employer.[490]

---

484. *Ibid.*, at paras 111(d), 132.
485. *Ibid.*, at paras 111(e), 132.
486. Database Registrar Guideline, 5/2017, *Workplace Surveillance* (2017).
487. *Ibid.*, at ss 15–17.
488. *Ibid.*, at ss 18–25.
489. *Ibid.*, at s. 29.
490. *Ibid.*, at s. 31.

485. These decisions have guided legislatures in additional contexts. For example, Amendment 33 to the Public Health Ordinance (No. 40), 1940, added a framework for the installation of CCTV cameras in geriatric hospitals, following the above principles insofar as the employees of the hospital are concerned.

§4. Monitoring of Employee IT Equipment

486. In a case challenging an employer's processing of personal data by way of monitoring the IT equipment of its employees, the National Labour Court considered the limitations of such processing. The Court generally acknowledged the employer's prerogative to control its IT systems and protect its systems from harm and misuse by employees. However, the Court emphasized the importance of employee privacy, stating that 'due to the augmented duties applicable to the parties to employment relationship, labour law has granted an increased value to the constitutional-objective of employee privacy'.[491] The Court applied the proportionality and transparency principles to such circumstances and provided for certain limitation on such processing and explicitly based its ruling on the WP29 guidelines on employee privacy.[492]

487. First, the Court determined that such processing should be established by written policy and code of conduct for the use of IT systems communicated to all employees monitored, explaining the nature of processing of personal data and that their IT equipment will be monitored by the employer.[493]

488. Second, the monitoring should be limited to circumstances giving rise to a clearly legitimate interest of the employer, such as potential fraud, breaches of confidentiality, or harm to the employer's assets.[494]

489. Third, the Court explained that if personal correspondence is identified in such monitoring, whether within the employee's professional IT equipment or in personal folders, viewing and processing such personal correspondence is always subject to a separate, explicit, informed, and freely given consent of the employee.[495] This may be a high threshold, especially in fraud-related circumstances where the cooperation of the employee is unlikely. Following the rulings of the National Labour Court, lower courts issued orders, allowing employers to search

491. *Issakov-Inbar*, at para. 12.
492. *Ibid.*, at para. 14 ('Workers do not abandon their right to privacy and data protection every morning at the entrance to the workplace. They do have a legitimate expectation of a certain degree of privacy in the workplace as they develop a significant part of their relationships with other human beings within the workplace.')
493. *Issakov-Inbar*, at para. 24.
494. *Ibid.*, at para. 27.
495. *Ibid.*, at para. 41.

personal correspondence of employees suspected of fraud, breaches of confidentiality, or other violations of the duty of loyalty.[496]

§5. BIOMETRIC DATA OF EMPLOYEES

490. The National Labour Court addressed employees' biometric data in circumstances where a municipality required educational employees to provide their fingerprint sample for use in an attendance system identifying the employee by her fingerprint. The system did not store the fingerprint image itself, rather only the mathematical hash of such image to allow for future identification, and thus the municipality argued that no biometric data was collected. Given that the cause of action was privacy infringement under section 2(9) of the PPA, the Court had to decide whether biometric data is a 'person's private affairs', and ruled in the affirmative.

491. The Court first determined that the fact that a fingerprint is initially collected to create the hash meant that biometric data was being processed at least for a limited time. With this in mind, and applying the legitimate interest and proportionality tests, the Court determined that such processing for attendance purposes could only be lawful subject to an explicit written consent of the employees to such processing while being provided an alternative identification methods.[497]

§6. LOCATION DATA OF EMPLOYEES

492. While the PPA does not explicitly acknowledge location data as either 'data' or the 'private affairs of a person,' the terms used therein, courts, including the Supreme Court, have determined that location data can reveal such private affairs of a person and could be considered personal data.[498]

493. In this context, the PP Authority published draft guidelines on the collection and processing of location data by employers in employment contexts.[499] Applying the criteria adopted by the National Labour Court discussed above, the Authority explained that such processing should be for a strictly legitimate interest of the employer and subject to proportionality and transparency vis-à-vis the employees. The Authority clarified that such legitimate interest will seldom exist for employees who work regularly in the same physical workplace, and that, while it

---

496. *See, e.g.*, LD (Nazareth, Regional Labour Court) 2684-03-16 *Koritani v. Zadok* (2017); LD (Tel Aviv, Regional Court) 18279-06-16 *Expo Management Ltd. v. Cohen* (2020).

497. *Qalansawe*, at paras 47,111–113, 132.

498. HCJ 6732/20 *ACRI v. The Knesset* (2021); AC (Tel Aviv, Admin. Court) 28857-06-17 *Caregiving Companies Association v. Ministry of Defence* (2019).

499. Privacy Protection Authority, Legal Opinion, *Collection of Employee Location Data by Employers Using Dedicated Applications and Vehicle Tracking Systems* (August 2021).

may be legitimate for field employees, the employer must first consider non-location-data alternatives, and if none are available restrict the collection of location data to the specific timeframe in which it is strictly necessary.[500]

500. *Caregiving Companies Association*, at para. 16.3; MP 5298/09 (Tel Aviv, Labour Court) *Rubin v. Oil and Energy Infrastructure Company* (2009).

Chapter 5. Processing for Scientific Research, Public Archiving and Statistical Purposes

§1. Scientific Research

494. The PPA does not contain any direct reference to scientific research processing. Thus, regular rules about data protection apply.[501] In specific cases, such as medical or genetic research, additional, specific rules apply. If the processing of data for research purposes is also a violation of traditional privacy torts, then the defences listed in section 18 and discussed above,[502] may be applicable. Note that these defences focus mostly on publication, rather than the collection or processing of the data.

495. When the scientific research conducted contains health data, the Patients' Rights Act, 1996 should be consulted, in addition to the PPA. The Patients' Rights Act contains a general duty of confidentiality regarding medical data (section 19), but it allows transferring medical data to other parties in some cases, two of which are relevant for academic processing. First, medical data can be transferred to another party with the patient's consent (section 20(a)(1)), and second, it is permitted to hand medical data for the purpose of publication in a scientific journal, or for purposes of research or teaching according to the Minister of Health's instructions, as long as identifying data is not revealed (section 20(a)(7), and section 32(4)). As of September 2022, no such instructions were issued.

496. Medical research conducted in hospitals is subject to an additional legal regime, of the Helsinki Ethical Principles for Medical Research Involving Human Subjects, which were integrated in Israeli law by way of regulations in 1980.[503]

497. Research of genetic data is subject to specific rules, under the GDA.[504] Such research is permitted only if the study was approved (section 3(c) of the GDA). Informed consent for DNA sampling for research should be in writing (section 11(b)). The GDA waives the consent requirement (under section 11) and the duty to notify the subject (under section 12) when the genetic data is used for research, that earned approval, which is based only on unidentified DNA samples, or de-identified samples, if re-identification is impossible 'in any manner' (section 13). Retention of genetic data is permitted, if identifying data was removed, unless the subject has consented in writing to the retention of identified samples (section 15(b)(2)). The General Director of the Ministry of Health is authorized to issue rules

---

501. Higher education institutions enjoy academic freedom, including regarding research, *see* Council for Higher Education Act, 1958, s. 15. However, this freedom is constrained by various laws and regulations regarding research in human subjects, as well as the PPA, regarding data subjects, as explained in this chapter. *See, e.g.*, Carmi, *supra* n. 109 1306.

502. *See* Part IX, Ch. 1.

503. People's Health Regulations (Medical Research Involving Human Subjects), 1980. Carmi, *supra* n. 109, at 1314.

504. For background and discussion, *see* Part I, Ch. 4, and discussion in Carmi, *supra* n. 109, at 1397–1408.

as to such retention (section 15(c)). Similarly, the holder of genetic data may transfer it to another party, for teaching, research, or publication in a scientific journal, if the research was approved, and if the data were transferred without identifying information or that the participant has consented, in writing, to such transfer, prior to the transfer (section 23). There are further rules regarding minors (sections 24(4), 26(a), 26(b)). Security bodies may use DNA samples that they possess for research related to forensic identification, intelligence gathering for national security purposes, and identification of bodies (section 32(a)(4)), or, for any other purpose – with the written consent of the person (section 32(a)(5)).

498. Research of umbilical cord blood is regulated in the Umbilical Cord Blood (Public Repository) Regulations, 2012.[505] A party who may consent to the collection and retention of the blood in the first place, may provide consent for using the blood for research, but if the sample cannot be frozen and stored, and if the research was approved (section 18).

§2. Public Archiving

499. The Archives Act, 1955, regulates the preservation of archival material, defined there as any material held by a state organ. Section 10(a) of this Act states that 'Every person may review archival material deposited in the State Archive, but this right may be limited by regulations.' Such regulations were issued, and they contain limiting access for the purpose of protecting privacy of people who may be mentioned therein, for seventy years.[506] The regulations refer to the PPA. The seventy-year period may be shortened in some cases. The regulations extend this protection also to deceased people.[507]

500. The Supreme Court addressed some cases in which access was limited for national security reasons,[508] but no cases regarding privacy were found.

§3. Statistical Purposes

501. The PPA does not address the issue of processing personal data for statistical purposes in a dedicated manner. Therefore, the general provisions of the PPA apply to such processing and consent or legal authorization remain the sole lawful ground for processing.

505. T. Trigger, *The Regulation of Fertility Services in Israel, in Regulating Regulation: Law and Policy* 269 (Y. Blank, D. Levi-Faur & R. Kreitner eds, Tel Aviv U. Press 2016) [Hebrew].
506. *See* Archives Regulation (Access to Archival Material Deposited in the State Archive), 2010, s. 8(b)(2).
507. Archives Regulation, s. 8(c)(2).
508. HCJ 15/19 *Hazkani v. Head of the Israel Security Service* (2021); HCJ 3345/19 *Kaplan v. State Archive* (2021).

502. Under the Israeli Statistics Ordinance [New Version], 1972, the Central Statistics Bureau (CSB), a statutory body established under the Ordinance, has the authority to collect data for statistical purposes, as well as compel any person or entity to disclose data for statistical purposes.[509] Identifiable data collected by the CSB is subject to statutory confidentiality and cannot be admitted as evidence in any proceedings.[510]

509. Statistics Ordinance [New Version], 1972, ss 11, 13.
510. *Ibid.*, ss 17, 19.

Part X. Specific Data Protection Regimes

Chapter 1. Obligation of Professional Secrecy

503. Israeli law acknowledges statutory secrecy and confidentiality obligations with respect to certain professions.

504. Attorney-client privilege is protected under Israeli law.[511] Generally, only the client may waive the privilege, and any information provided under such privilege that are related to the legal services obtained provided by the attorney cannot be disclosed in legal proceedings.[512] The privilege does not apply to future criminal intentions of the client or to ongoing criminal offences.[513]

505. Medical privilege and secrecy are protected under Israeli law. Caretakers, defined broadly as physical and mental health professionals, are bound by professional secrecy and cannot disclose any information obtained from their patients without the approval of the patient, if otherwise required to do so under applicable law or with the approval of ethical committees for public health and safety purposes or for anonymous scientific research.[514] Medical caretakers, psychologists and social workers cannot be compelled to provide such professional secrets in court, unless a court issues a compelling order after balancing legitimate necessity and the interest of secrecy.[515]

506. The law acknowledges privilege in legal proceedings over confessions made to religious priests and are bound by secrecy under the rules of the applicable religion.[516]

511. Israeli Bar Association Act, 1961, s. 90; Evidence Ordinance [New Version], 1971, s. 48.
512. Evidence Ordinance [New Version], 1971, s. 48.
513. MCrP 7064/08 *State of Israel v. Berko*, 63(2) PD 453 (2009). *See also* I. Amit, *Privileges and Protected Interests Discovery and Review Procedures in Civil and Criminal Law* 451–504 (Nevo 2021) [Hebrew].
514. Patients' Rights Act, 1996, ss 19–20.
515. Evidence Ordinance [New Version], 1971, ss 49–50A; Amit, *supra* n. 510, at 613–630, 639–664; HCJ 447/72 *Ismahovitz v. Baruch* 27(2) PD 253 (1973); Crim. A. 8974/07 *Lin v. State of Israel* (2010).
516. Evidence Ordinance [New Version], 1971, s. 51.

507. The Supreme Court has acknowledged a limited source-journalist privilege.[517] This privilege can, however, be waived by the court under special justifications at its discretion.[518]

508. The PPA and other privacy-related legislation and case law anchored these obligations. The PPA lists, as two of the privacy torts, the breach of a duty of secrecy 'laid down by law in respect to a person's private affairs' (section 2(7)), and the breach of a duty made by an express or implicit agreement (section 2(8)). For example, a photojournalist took a photo of an ultraorthodox man at the background of a provocative advertisement of a woman in a sexist position and promised not to publish it – yet, he did publish it in a national newspaper. The Supreme Court ruled that the broken promise infringed privacy under section 2(8).[519]

509. The Criminal Procedure Act (Enforcement Powers – Communications Data), 2007 Act contains special rules allowing the police and other law enforcement agencies to obtain communications data from telecommunications providers under a court order (section 3). Section 4 of the Act allows a certified officer to mandate disclosure of communications data in urgent cases without a court order. The Supreme Court ruled that when such administrative power is used without a court order to disclose the communication data of a journalist, this could result in compromising journalistic privilege. Accordingly, the Court ruled that this administrative power be deemed constitutional only subject to public police guidelines assuring that when a journalist is concerned, such administrative power is not be used.[520]

517. MP 86/298 *Citrin v. Disciplinary Court for the Tel Aviv District of the Bar Association*, 41(2) PD 337 (1987).

518. For elaboration, *see* S. Yeroslavsky Karni & T. Schwarz Altschuler, *Regulating Journalistic Privilege*, Policy Research No. 104 (Israeli Democratic Institute 2015) [Hebrew].

519. LCA 6902/06 *Zadik v. Haaretz Newspaper Publishing Ltd.*, 63(1) PD 52 (2008).

520. HCJ 3809/08 *ACRI v. Israeli Police*, 65 PD 694, 725 (2012). *See also* Police Guidelines 03.344.306, s. 7(b)(5).

Chapter 2. Churches and Religious Associations

510. While various religious associations are active in Israel, especially in the three leading religions of Judaism, Islam, and Christianity, there is no reference in Israeli law to special rules pertaining to data processing by such religious institutions.

511. In several important issues, Israel does not separate state and religion. Thus, for some civil issues, religious institutions have statutory exclusive jurisdiction, such as for marriage and divorce.[521] However, most institutions administering such civil matters are public bodies and thus operate by authorizing laws and are subject to both administrative and constitutional law, as well as to the PPA.[522] Therefore, their personal data processing practices have to meet both the requirements of the PPA, which also apply to public bodies and governmental branches (section 24), as well as administrative law principles such as proportionality and reasonableness, which provide a stricter framework for the processing of personal data and its legitimacy.

512. In a leading case, the Supreme Court reviewed a decision of the High Rabbinical Court to allow evidence – intimate photographs taken by a husband, of his wife with another man, without their consent, in a house owned by the husband and the wife.[523] The evidence were highly important under Jewish law, to prove adultery. Courts have discretion whether to exclude or allow evidence that harms privacy (section 32), and the question was whether this behaviour was harmful to privacy. The Rabbinical Court emphasized that a married couple does not have privacy vis-à-vis each other. The Supreme Court disagreed. The Court ruled that every person has an 'autonomic unit' of privacy, regardless of the place (echoing the American ruling that the Fourth Amendment protects 'people, not places'),[524] even though the parties were still married at the time. The Supreme Court further ruled that privacy law applies and is binding in the religious courts.

521. *See* Palestine Order in Council 1922, ss 51(1)–57.
522. HCJ 7237/95 *Arar v. The Minister of Religious Affairs*, 51(1) PD 193 (1997).
523. HCJ 6650/04 *Doe v. Regional Rabbinical Court, Netanya*, 61(1) PD 581 (2006).
524. *Katz v. United States*, 389 U.S. 347, 351 (1967).

Chapter 3. Law Enforcement Agencies

§1. Introduction

513. Law enforcement agencies enjoy various powers in order to perform their tasks; these powers often violate privacy. Given that the law enforcement agencies are public bodies, their actions are subject to administrative law principles, and when their actions affect privacy, also to constitutional law.

514. The Basic Law: Human Dignity and Liberty protects privacy both in a general manner (Article 7(a): 'Every person has a right to privacy and to intimacy in his life'), and in specific cases, regarding entering into private premises (Article 7(b)), conducting a search in private premises, the body or personal effects (Article 7(c)), and the confidentiality of communications (Article 7(d)).[525] Privacy, like other rights protected under the Basic Law, is not absolute, and can be limited. Article 8 is a limitations clause: 'One is not to violate the rights accorded by this Basic Law save by means of a law that corresponds to the values of the State of Israel, which serves an appropriate purpose, and to an extent that does not exceed what is required, or on the basis of a law, as aforementioned, by force of an explicit authorization therein.'

515. Accordingly, for a law enforcement agency to be able to perform an action that violates privacy, it should meet the requirements set in the Basic Law. There are several laws that authorize such activities, and there are some police practices which are currently (as of December 2022) challenged and there are pending petitions in their regard.[526] Where the Court found that the police lacked statutory authority, it restrained the police activity.[527]

516. This chapter discusses some exemptions that law enforcement agencies enjoy under the PPA, data transfers to these agencies, the law regarding various searches, and other police activities.

§2. PPA Exemptions for Law Enforcement Agencies

517. When the data controller (database owner, in the PPA's terms) is a security agency, some data subjects' rights are limited. Security agencies are defined in

525. *See also* Part I, Ch. 1.

526. *See* HCJ 641/21 *Association for Civil Rights in Israel (ACRI) v. Israel Police* (submitted in January 2021), where ACRI challenges the police use of a technology called Hawkeye, which comprises of cameras placed in various roads and highways, that can automatically read license plates, and check the data in police databases, even when there is no specific suspicion.

527. *See, e.g.*, HCJ 6824/07 *Manna v. Tax Authority*, 64(2) PD 479 (2010), regarding data transfers from police to tax collectors, and HCJ 4455/19 *Tebeka Advocacy for Equality & Justice for Ethiopian Israelis v. Israel Police* (2021), regarding processing data collected from people where there is no suspicion against them.

section 19(c), and include the police, IDF intelligence unit, the ISA, the Mossad, and the Witness Protection Authority.

518. Security agencies are required to register their databases with the Database Registrar as they meet several of the conditions set in section 8(c), most directly, they are public bodies (section 8(c)(4)), and in addition, we can presume that these databases contain data about more than 10,000 people, that the information was not delivered by the subjects, and that it contains sensitive data. The registrar is open to the public (section 12(a)), but under section 12(c) (which refers to section 9((b)), the security agencies' registration contains some details which are not open to the public: The kinds of data, details about transferring the data to third countries, and data about the sources of the data.

519. Security agencies, as well as additional agencies such as the Israel Prison Authority and Tax Authority, are exempt from enabling data subjects' right to access their personal data (section 13(e)).[528] The PPA further exempts databases about investigations and law enforcement agencies determined in an Order by the Minister of Justice.[529] While not explicitly stated in the PPA, the exemption from enabling access also means that it is in practice more difficult to rectify incorrect data. Regarding criminal records, the Criminal Data and Rehabilitation Act, 2019 regulates the retention of such data, access thereto, its transfer to other bodies, corrections, and expungement.

520. The various defences set in section 18, such as acting in good faith in circumstances where the infringer was under a legal, moral, social, or professional obligation (section 18(2)) may also apply to law enforcement activities.[530]

521. Section 19 contains broader exemptions. The first (section 19(a)) states that 'No person shall bear responsibility under this Law for an act which he is empowered to do by law.' The second exemption is specific for security agencies: 'A security authority or a person employed by it or acting on its behalf shall bear no responsibility under this Law for an infringement reasonably committed within the scope of their functions and for the purpose of carrying them out' (section 19(b)). While the police tend to cite this exemption as a statutory empowerment to act, ex ante, in a manner that infringes privacy, the Supreme Court clarified that the exemption applied only when there was a prior, separate authorization to act and that it did not create such authorization. The Chief Justice emphasized that the exemption negated a cause of action under the PPA, but did not contain an all-embracing exemption from respecting constitutional privacy.[531]

528. For the right to access, *see* Part IV, Ch. 2.
529. Such an order was issued in 1987, adding the Ministry of Defence and some military industries. *See* Privacy Protection Regulations (Determining Databases that Contain Data not to be Revealed), 1987.
530. *See also* Part VIII, Ch. 6.
531. *Tebeka*, at para. 33.

§3. Law Enforcement Access to Personal Data Held by Other Authorities

522. Various laws permit public data controllers to hand over data to law enforcement agencies. For example, the Chief of the Police – and whomever the Chief authorized – may access the national population registry;[532] the Inclusion of Biometric Identifiers and Biometric Data in Identification Documents and a Database, 2009 authorizes the transfer of biometric data from the central biometric database to a police officer when the officer has acquired biometric data from the person;[533] a court may order the transfer of data to the police for investigations, authentication of identity (including for identifying a body) or transfer of data to a law enforcement agency abroad.[534]

§4. Search

523. Several laws authorize law enforcement agencies to conduct searches and seizures. One set of laws addresses electronic communications.[535] Other laws contain detailed rules about police searches of according to a judicial warrant, of private premises,[536] 'computer material',[537] searches without a warrant in special cases,[538] external search on the body of suspects,[539] or detainees,[540] additional external searches,[541] and internal searches, such as blood retrieval, gynaecologist test, or body imaging.[542] These laws contain detailed procedures about court warrants, procedures for conducting the searches, retention, and use of the data.[543]

524. Evidence that was obtained by infringing privacy is inadmissible in judicial proceedings (section 32), unless one of three situations occur: That the subject has consented to the submission; that the court has discretion over the matter; and that if the infringer enjoyed a defence or an exemption. Note that in the context of

532. Population Registry Act, 1965, s. 31(4).
533. Inclusion of Biometric Identifiers and Biometric Data in Identification Documents and a Database Act, 2009, s. 16.
534. *Ibid.*, s. 17. There are additional specific rules permitting data transfer when the police investigates fraud regarding biometric documents (s. 18), and limitations on onward biometric data transfers (s. 19).
535. *See* Part I, Ch. 3.
536. Criminal Procedure Ordinance (Arrest and Search) [New Version], 1969, s. 23.
537. *Ibid.*, s. 23A.
538. *Ibid.*, s. 25.
539. *Ibid.*, s. 29.
540. *Ibid.*, s. 22.
541. Criminal Procedure Act (Enforcement Powers – Searching the Body and Retrieving Identification Means), 1996, s. 3.
542. *Ibid.*, s. 4.
543. For discussion, *see* A. Harpaz with M. Golan, *Law and Policing – Human Rights and Police Powers* (Israel Democracy Institute 2018) [Hebrew].

unlawful wiretapping, inadmissibility is absolute.[544] A 2022 amendment to the Evidence Ordinance broadened judicial discretion to exclude evidence in criminal trials for various other situations of unlawful obtaining of evidence.[545]

544. Wiretapping Act, 1979, s. 13.
545. An Act to Amend the Evidence Ordinance (No. 19), 2022. The Act clarifies, in the newly added s. 56A(b), that it did not affect other legislative exclusion rules.

Chapter 4. National Security Services

§1. Introduction

525. Israel has several security agencies, other than the IDF. The ISA, a.k.a. General Security Service, *Shin Bet*, or *Shaback*) is the internal security agency, and is regulated by the Israel Security Agency Act, 2002; the Mossad is Israel's national intelligence agency, which is mentioned in several laws, including the PPA, but is not regulated in a *sui generis* law. There are additional security bodies, such as the Director of Security at the Ministry of Defence (a.k.a. *Malmab*), which operates within the Ministry.

526. Other than the ISA Act and the PPA, there is a web of legislation that together regulate the powers of security agencies in privacy and data protection-related matters. Some of these laws were discussed in the previous chapter, as they bundle together law enforcement and security agencies, as well as the overarching Basic Law: Human Dignity and Liberty. However, the web also has some holes. As a detailed comparative study has shown, several major issues are left unregulated:[546] There is no direct legislative reference to bulk collection of data; extra-territorial activities of security bodies is also unclear; Israeli law does not regulate the retention of communications or communications data (although as we explain below, there may be such secret regulations), and there is no clear regulation of data processing.

§2. Data Gathering

527. The ISA Act authorizes the agency to gather information, share it with other bodies, in addition to all police powers (section 8). Searches at border points are authorized as well, including covert searches (section 9(b)). The Prime Minister may permit covert searches in private premises and vehicles (section 10(a)), and the Head of the ISA may do so in urgent cases (section 10(b)).

§3. Exemptions

528. The exemptions discussed in the previous chapter, regarding law enforcement agencies, apply to security agencies, including the exemption from making available to the public some elements about their databases (PPA, section 12), and from enabling access (section 13).

529. The ISA and its employees are exempt from liability for privacy violations when acting under sufficient authorization, and in a reasonable manner (section 19(b)).

546. A. Cahane with Y. Shany, *Regulation of Online Surveillance in Israeli Law and Comparative Law* (Israel Democracy Institute 2019) [Hebrew].

§4. COMMUNICATION DATA

530. Under the Communications Act (Telecommunication and Broadcasting), 1982 ('Telecom Act'), the communication service providers may operate only if they have received a license. Section 13(b) authorizes the Prime Minister may instruct the licensees to adjust their technological systems to enable the security agencies listed in the Act, access. The agencies are the IDF, ISA, Mossad, Israel Police, and Israel Prison Authority (section 13(a)). Such instructions are to be kept secret (section 13(d)). The ISA Act supplements this power, by authorizing the Prime Minister to determine that kinds of data held by communication service providers are needed to the ISA to perform its tasks (section 11(b)), and authorized the head of the ISA to permit such uses (section 11(c)). Related rules are also secret (section 19(a)(1)).

531. The Wiretapping Act, 1979 authorizes the Prime Minister and the Minister of Defence to issue wiretapping orders for national security purposes, and details relevant procedures (section 4), and further authorizes the Head of the ISA to issue urgent orders, for no longer than forty-eight hours (section 5).

532. The extent of use of this legal arrangement is not public. However, at the outbreak of the COVID-19 Pandemic, a journalist report revealed that since 2002, the ISA operates a technological system, known as 'the tool' that enables identifying, in real time, the location of cellular holders.[547] The government ordered the ISA to use its tool for the purpose of contact tracing. Initially, the order was made via emergency orders, then a special Act was enacted by the Knesset, which served as an ongoing legal basis for this operation, for more than a year. The Act expired, and with the appearance of the Omicron variant, the government resorted once again to emergency orders.

533. The use of the ISA tool for contact tracing was challenged in the Supreme Court three times.[548] The first case focused on the authorizing anchor, and the court limited the duration of the use and urged the government to initiate legislation, which it did.[549] A second case challenged the new Act. The Court limited its use to cases in which infected people refused to cooperate in an epidemiological inquiry.[550] A third case approved the five-day use of the tool in light of Omicron.[551]

547. R. Bergman & I. Shvartztuch, *The 'Tool': The ISA's Secret Data Base*, Yediot Ahronot, 25 Mar. 2020 [Hebrew], at https://www.yediot.co.il/articles/0,7340,L-5701611,00.html.

548. For discussion, *see* M. Birnhack, *Privacy in Crisis: Constitutional Engineering and Privacy Engineering*, 24 Law & Gov. Israel 149 (2022) [Hebrew].

549. HCJ 2109/20 *Ben-Meir v. Prime Minister* (2020).

550. HCJ 6732/20 *ACRI v. The Knesset* (2021).

551. HCJ 8196/21 *ACRI v. The Government* (2021).

Chapter 5. Other Specific Regimes

§1. INTRODUCTION

534. Previous parts reviewed various specific regimes pertaining to the processing of personal data. These included biometric data,[552] genetic data,[553] medical data,[554] financial data,[555] electronic communications,[556] law enforcement,[557] employment relationships,[558] and more. In this final chapter we discuss several additional specific regimes which were not addressed earlier.

§2. CCTV CAMERAS AND MASS SURVEILLANCE

535. The context of processing of personal data through CCTV cameras and other public mass surveillance means is addressed in several venues of Israeli law.

536. Although, generally, the privacy tort part of the PPA does not prohibit taking pictures or filming individuals in the public sphere, in 2012, the PP Authority issued guidelines explaining that retaining such footage in digitized form is subject to the data protection provisions of the PPA and is thus subject to the notification duties of section 11 of the PPA and requires database registration.[559] In addition, the Authority explained that given the potential privacy harms of mass monitoring, any organization installing CCTV cameras in public must meet legitimacy and proportionality criteria for their operation, conduct a privacy impact assessment to address the privacy risks and their mitigation, provide transparent notification to the public, as well as meet all data subject rights, and establish proportionate data retention policies for the footage collected and stored.[560]

537. The Authority also determined that if such cameras are installed by private organizations who require consent as a legal basis for processing, meeting the foregoing criteria may establish adequate informed implicit consent. However, in the context of public bodies, in addition to meeting the foregoing requirements, an explicit statutory authorization must be demonstrated for the data collection to be lawful.

538. The practice of the Israeli police and municipalities to install CCTV cameras for the purpose of enforcing transportation regulations was challenged in

552. *See* discussion in Part I, Ch. 4 above.
553. *See* discussion in Part I, Ch. 4 above.
554. *See* discussion in Part I, Ch. 4 above.
555. *See* discussion in Part I, Ch. 4 above.
556. *See* discussion in Part I, Ch. 3 above.
557. *See* discussion in Part X, Ch. 3 above.
558. *See* discussion in Part IX, Ch. 4 above.
559. Database Registrar Guideline, 4/2012 *Use of Security and Surveillance Cameras Database's Captured Images* (2012).
560. *Ibid.*, at s. 3.

several judicial proceedings, arguing that no explicit law authorized such conduct.[561] In 2022, the Supreme Court issued an interim order with respect to a police camera system, Hawkeye (*Ein HaNetz*, in Hebrew), which allegedly constantly monitors all vehicles in Israel, due to allegations that such conduct is without legal authority and is unconstitutional due to its privacy harms.[562]

539. In other contexts, explicit laws authorize or even mandate the installation of CCTV cameras. For example, the Installation of Cameras for Protection Infants in Day-care Institutions Act, 2018, was enacted at the backdrop of public outrage following a sequence of child abuse cases in private day-care institutions. The Act mandates the installation of CCTV cameras in regulated day-cares and requires due notification of the existence of such cameras, their coverage, and purpose of use.[563] It also requires that the cameras are installed in a manner fulfilling the purpose of the Act while preserving, to the extent possible, the privacy of the infants and staff members.[564] The Act also regulates the retention period of the footage with a limitation of thirty days or otherwise as set forth in regulations,[565] and provides a mechanism for viewing the footage by law enforcement agencies or under a court order.[566]

540. The General Director of the MoE issued guidelines on the use of CCTV cameras in educational institutions in 2015.[567] The guidelines limit the purposes for installing such cameras. One purpose allowed is promoting safety and prohibiting dangerous or illegal conduct in schools.[568] The decision whether to install cameras for such purpose remains with school principals if they are convinced that the cameras are necessary to achieve the above purposes.[569] Another lawful purpose is protecting the educational facility and any school assets after-school hours. The installation decision for this purpose remains with the owner or operator of the educational facility.[570] A final lawful purpose is promoting the security in schools and kindergartens. In these cases, the decision remains with the owner of the facility, the local municipality, or law enforcement agencies.[571]

541. In any of the foregoing circumstances, the MoE Guidelines require that the installation of the cameras considers privacy of both students and staff, privacy mitigating measures such as the filming angles and locations of the cameras, and that

561. CC (Tel Aviv, Magistrate) 72118789 *State of Israel v. Mizrahi* (2018).
562. HCJ 641/21 *Association for Civil Rights in Israel v. Israel Police* (2021) (Petitioner's pleadings).
563. Cameras for Protection Infants in Day-care Institutions Act, 2018, ss 3–4.
564. *Ibid.*, s. 5.
565. *Ibid*, s. 6.
566. *Ibid*, s. 7.
567. 65/9(a) Ministry of Education Circular, Cameras in Educational Institutions – Regulating Their Introduction and Installation Procedure (3 May 2015); M. Birnhack & L. Perry-Hazan, *Privacy, CCTV, and School Surveillance in the Shadow of Imagined Law*, 50(2) Law & Soc'y Rev. 415 (2016).
568. Guidelines, *ibid.*, s. 2.1.
569. *Ibid.*, s. 2.2.
570. MoE Guidelines, *ibid.*, ss 3.1–3.2.
571. *Ibid.*, ss 4.1–4.2.

the retention of footage be restricted, in some cases to a maximum of three days. The guidelines also limit the individuals who may have access permissions to live footage and to recorded footage and the circumstances in which viewing of the footage is allowed.

§3. Credit Scoring and Financial Information Services

542. The Knesset enacted laws and regulations pertaining to centralized credit scoring, open banking, and open financial information services in recent years.[572] Such laws include specific data protection provisions and have created a complementary regime for such purposes of personal data processing. Specifically:

543. The Credit Data Act, 2016, established a centralized credit score database operated and controlled by the BoI. Various types of financial institutions and credit providers are mandated to contribute data pertaining to their credit-related transactions to the Credit Database. From the BoI perspective, the Act requires the appointment of a DPO which is a BoI employee, limits the purposes for which the Credit Database will operate and sets forth security and operation requirements for the management of such database.

544. The Act limits data transfers from the Credit Database and permits them only to certified and licensed credit bureaus (sections 26–32). The Act creates a strong and restricted purpose limitation for any data obtained from the Credit Database to prevent data enrichment (section 25), and only allows data transfers to data subject who requested credit reports about themselves or to credit providers who obtained the consent of such data subject to obtain a credit score for a specific credit transaction. The Act also mandates specific retention periods and prohibits the use of outdated or inaccurate credit data.

545. A parallel regime was established in the Financial Information Services Act, 2021. The Act aims at providing open access to banking and financial information to allow various service providers and technology companies to offer smart financial management solutions for individuals. The Act makes such financial data available upon demand only to licensed organizations meeting various requirements, including meeting adequate privacy and data protection standards (section 4(a)). The Act also restricts the processing of such open financial data to circumstances where the service provider obtained and explicit written consent of the data subject (section 26), with a strong purpose limitation for providing the financial information services or certain limited peripheral services only (section 25(a)). The Act also provides for a maximum retention period of such data of up to seven years, with an exception for data that is required to be retained for longer period under other laws or for legal claims defence purposes (sections 27(b)–(c)).

572. *See, e.g.*, the Credit Data Act, 2016 and the Financial Information Services Act, 2021.

§4. PROCESSING OF MINORS' DATA

546. The PPA does not provide special treatment for the processing of children's personal data. Thus, without a designated framework, the processing of children's personal data is subject to all provisions of the PPA that apply to the processing of adults' personal data.

547. However, given that the primary lawful basis for processing of personal data under the PPA is consent, general principles of legal capacity and guardianship apply to the processing of minors' personal data.

548. The Legal Capacity and Guardianship Act, 1962, sets the general framework for legal capacity in Israel. Section 3 of the Act provides that any person under the age of 18 is a minor. The legal actions of a minor, as a general principle, require his or her parent or legal guardian's consent (section 4). Such consent could be general, specific, in advance, or in retrospect, and can be rescinded if the legal action was not yet performed.[573] The legal actions of a minor that were made without the consent of his or her parents or guardians is voidable (section 5).

549. The Act, however, provides that despite the foregoing, two types of legal actions could be valid even absent parental or guardian consent: (i) The action is customary for minors of that certain age; (ii) The other party to the action did not know or should have known that the first party is a minor (section 6). Such actions could only be voidable if causing substantive harm to the minor.

550. Courts have not yet addressed the qualifications of section 6 of the Act in privacy or data protection circumstances. In other cases, courts have determined that minor of a relatively older age were capable of performing legal actions such as purchasing of mobile devices and communication plans.[574] These qualifications may, in certain circumstances, render some processing of personal data of minors lawful even absent parental consent.

573. For a discussion on a minor's right to withdraw from parental consent, *see* S. Calev, *'I Decide on Me' – Children's Privacy in the Digital Era and the Right to Withdraw from Parental Consent*, 41 TAU L. Rev. 112 (2018) [Hebrew].

574. CC (Rishon LeTzion, Magistrate) 3130-06-11 *Yitzhaki v. Cellcom Israel Ltd.* (2012); OM (Haifa, Magistrate) 54502-06-*16 Yunas v. Kafri Agencies Ltd.* (2017).

Selected Bibliography

Amit, I. *Evidentiary Privileges and Protected Interests: Discovery Proceedings in Civil and Criminal Law*. Nevo, 2021.

Arbel, Y. & T. Schwartz Altshuler. *Information Wants to Be Free: Implementing the Freedom of Information Act in Israel*. Israel Democracy Institute, 2008 [Hebrew].

Barak, A. *Proportionality in Law*. Nevo, 2010 [Hebrew].

Barak-Erez, D. *Administrative Law*. Nevo, 2010–2017 [Hebrew].

Ben-Naftali, O., M. Sfard & H. Viterbo (eds). *The ABC of the OPT: A Legal Lexicon of the Israeli Control over the Occupied Palestinian Territory*. Cambridge University Press, 2018.

Birnhack, M. 'Consent and Control: The Theoretical Basis of the Right to Privacy'. *Law & Gov. Israel* 11 (2008): 11 [Hebrew].

Birnhack, M. *Private Space*. Bar-Ilan & Nevo, 2010 [Hebrew].

Birnhack, M. 'Surveillance at Work: Taylor, Bentham and the Right to Privacy'. *Labour, Society & Law* 12 (2010): 9 [Hebrew].

Birnhack, M. & L. Perry-Hazan. 'Privacy, CCTV, and School Surveillance in the Shadow of Imagined Law'. *Law & Soc. Rev.* 50(2) (2016): 415.

Birnhack, M. 'Privacy in Crisis: Constitutional Engineering and Privacy Engineering'. *Law & Gov. Israel* 24 (2022): 149 [Hebrew].

Birnhack, M. 'Privacy in Crisis: Constitutional Engineering and Privacy Engineering'. *Law & Government in Israel* 24 (2022): 149 [Hebrew].

Birnhack, M. 'From Urich to Pegasus: On Constitutional Privacy in Police Investigations'. ICON-S-IL BLOG (2022) [Hebrew].

Birnhack, M. *Constitutional Privacy*. Bar-Ilan & Nevo Press, 2023 [Hebrew].

Cahane A. with Y. Shany. *Regulation of Online Surveillance in Israeli Law and Comparative Law*. Israel Democracy Institute, 2019 [Hebrew].

Calev, S., '"I Decide on Me" – Children's Privacy in the Digital Era and the Right to Withdraw from Parental Consent'. *TAU L. Rev.* 41 (2018): 112.

Carmi, A. 1 *Health and Law*, edited by M.S. Wattad, 2nd edn. Nevo, 2013 [Hebrew].

Duke, S.A. 'Nontargets: Understanding the Apathy Towards the Israeli Security Agency's COVID-19 Surveillance'. *Surveillance and Society* 19(1) (2021): 114.

Ghanayim, K., M. Kremnitzer & B. Shnoor. *Libel Law de lege lata and lege ferenda*. 2nd edn. Sacher & Nevo, 2019 [Hebrew].

Gidron, T., 'Defamation Law in Turbulence: Does Israel Need "Libel Reform"?. *Isr. L. Rev.* 46(1) (2013): 95.

Selected Bibliography

Golan, T. 'The Examining and the Observing Eye: Regulation and Policing of Employee Behavior in the Workplace'. In *Regulating Regulation: Law and Policy*, edited by Y. Blank, D. Levi-Faur &. R. Kreitner. Tel Aviv U. Press, 2016, 515 [Hebrew].

Halm, E. *Privacy Law*. Perelshtein Genossar Press 2003 [Hebrew].

Harpaz, A. with M. Golan. *Law and Policing – Human Rights and Police Powers*. Israel Democracy Institute, 2018 [Hebrew].

Marciano, A. 'Israel's Biometric Project in Mainstream Israeli Press'. 2 *Law, Society & Culture* 237 (2019) [Hebrew].

Medina, B. *Human Rights Law in Israel*. Sacher Press, 2016 [Hebrew].

Morse, T., 'Covering the Dead'. *Journalism Studies* 15(1) (2014): 98.

Nahon, K. 'The Politics of the Biometric Database'. *Law, Society & Culture* 2 (2019): 271 [Hebrew].

Navot, S. 'Israel: Creating a Constitution – The Use of Foreign Precedents by the Supreme Court (1994–2010)'. In *The Use of Foreign Precedents by Constitutional Judges*, edited by T. Groppi & M. Ponthoreau. Hart Publishing, 2013, 129.

Rabin, Y. & R. Peled. 'The Constitutional Right to Receive Information'. In *The Dorner Book*, edited by S. Almog, D. Beinisch & Y. Rotem. Nevo, 2009, 463 [Hebrew].

Rachum-Twaig, O. 'Computerized Searches'. *Tel Aviv Law Review Forum* (2022) [Hebrew].

Ronen, Y. 'The Applicability of Basic Law: Human Dignity and Liberty in the West Bank'. *Sha'arey Mishpat* 7 (2014): 149 [Hebrew].

Shalev, C. 'Genetic Databases: Private and Public in Research and Development'. *Medicine & L.* 27 (2002): 70.

Shinar, A. 'Israel's External Constitution: Friends, Enemies, and the Constitutional / Administrative Law Distinction'. *Va. J. Inte'l L.* 57 (2018): 735.

Trigger, T. 'The Regulation of Fertility Services in Israel'. In *Regulating Regulation: Law and Policy*, edited by Y. Blank, D. Levi-Faur & R. Kreitner. Tel Aviv University Press, 2016 [Hebrew].

Yeroslavsky Karni, S. & T. Schwarz Altschuler. 'Regulating Journalistic Privilege, Policy Research No. 104. Israeli Democratic Institute, 2015 [Hebrew].

Index

The numbers here refer to paragraph numbers.

Index

Index

www.ingramcontent.com/pod-product-compliance
Lightning Source LLC
Chambersburg PA
CBHW071341230926
51846CB00002B/414
9789403535067